P9-CLD-336

4:09:43

MAR 2 0 2014

PRAISE FOR *4:09:43*

"Some would like to forget the horror of the 2013 Boston Marathon. However, many more of us would like to celebrate the unflinching runners, medical staff, and community of Boston for the courage and love they showed each other in marathon's time of greatest need. Hal Higdon's book 4:09:43 is full of inspiring personal stories that reflect how running's worst day may also have been its best."

Amby Burfoot
Boston Marathon Champion
Editor at Large, *Runner's World*

"We realize while reading the marathoners' own words why they will not be stopped by the bombings that took place. It's simple: Love is stronger than hate."

Bill Rodgers
Four-Time Boston and NYC Marathon Champion

"The Boston bombings broke the hearts of runners everywhere but only reinforced their spirit. Through the stories of some who were actually there, Hal Higdon tells how ordinary runners like us have become indomitable examples to the whole world."

Kathrine Switzer
First woman to officially run the Boston Marathon
Longtime TV commentator on the event
Author of *Marathon Woman*

"*Higdon's account avoids the political sensationalizing of the events of April 15, 2013. Instead, he tells the story of Boston through the eyes of dozens of participants, revealing what the event means to hundreds of thousands of runners and how the explosions of that day burst into this iconic event and experience. Read this book if you love Boston.*"

Jonathan Beverly
Editor in Chief, *Running Times*

"*I was there on April 15, 2013, a hundred yards beyond the finish line, when the bombs changed an annual ritual of personal achievement into a horror show. But I didn't see everything there was to see, didn't understand all the stories of bravery and loss happening on Boylston Street that day. No one person could, which is why this book is so valuable. It's the closest we can come to having been everywhere on that one terrible, miraculous day.*"

Peter Sagal
Host of NPR's *Wait Wait... Don't Tell Me*
2013 Boston Marathon Finisher

"*Hal Higdon has captured the absolute dichotomy that was the April 15 Boston Marathon, a very real Tale of Two Cities. It was the best of times and the worst of times, from the beautiful and uplifting marathon celebration that Boston is known for to an absolute day of fear, horror, and mayhem. Told through the emotional lens and perspective of actual runners and other witnesses to terror, the heartfelt story of the 117th running is a complex and sometimes contradictory series of emotions and is at once gripping, sensitive, and inspiring. Runners worldwide and all those who love the Boston Marathon will find 4:09:43 a compelling account of the many emotions of the day as well as a meaningful tribute to its greatness.*"

Guy Morse
Former Executive Director of the Boston Athletic Association
Organizer of the Boston Marathon, 1985 to 2012

"*Hal Higdon in* 4:09:43 *proves that the Boston Marathon consists of every runner in the race and every spectator along the course—and when you attack even one, you attack all.*"

Dave McGillivray
Boston Marathon Race Director

"*I can think of no one better equipped than Hal Higdon to tell this story. It is a story of the special kinship of all of us who have run that final straightaway down Boylston Street toward the finish of the Boston Marathon. And it is the story of how those two explosions were instantly and instinctively felt—from whatever distance we experienced them—to be an attack on all of us. This is an amazing story, skillfully woven together by one of our sport's great chroniclers.*"

John Parker
Author of *Once a Runner*

"*Hal Higdon uses social media and personal correspondence to compile a powerful narrative for the tragic 2013 Boston Marathon. The collection of essays in* 4:09:43 *is a tribute to a marathon that Higdon knows deeply.*"

Roger Robinson
Author of *Running in Literature*

"*He's run Boston 18 times with a PR of 2:21 and best finish of fifth place. He wrote the definitive history about the race,* Boston: A Century of Running, *as well as countless articles. His training programs have helped thousands of runners qualify for Boston. Now Hal has called on that long lifetime of experience to help us understand the events of the day and the bombing's aftermath. For runners everywhere it is a must-read.*"

Roy Benson
Author of *Heart Rate Training* and *Precision Running*

4:09:43

Boston 2013 Through the Eyes of the Runners

HAL HIGDON

Contributing Editor, *Runner's World*

Human Kinetics

ISBN-10: 1-4504-9710-1 (print)
ISBN-13: 978-1-4504-9710-7 (print)

Copyright © 2014 by Hal Higdon

All rights reserved. Except for use in a review, the reproduction or utilization of this work in any form or by any electronic, mechanical, or other means, now known or hereafter invented, including xerography, photocopying, and recording, and in any information storage and retrieval system, is forbidden without the written permission of the publisher.

Cover designer: Keith Blomberg
Photograph (cover): AP Photo/Elise Amendola
Printer: United Graphics

Human Kinetics books are available at special discounts for bulk purchase. Special editions or book excerpts can also be created to specification. For details, contact the Special Sales Manager at Human Kinetics.

Printed in the United States of America   10 9 8 7 6 5 4 3 2 1

The paper in this book is certified under a sustainable forestry program.

Human Kinetics
Website: www.HumanKinetics.com

United States: Human Kinetics
P.O. Box 5076
Champaign, IL 61825-5076
800-747-4457
e-mail: humank@hkusa.com

Canada: Human Kinetics
475 Devonshire Road Unit 100
Windsor, ON N8Y 2L5
800-465-7301 (in Canada only)
e-mail: info@hkcanada.com

Europe: Human Kinetics
107 Bradford Road
Stanningley
Leeds LS28 6AT, United Kingdom
+44 (0) 113 255 5665
e-mail: hk@hkeurope.com

Australia: Human Kinetics
57A Price Avenue
Lower Mitcham, South Australia 5062
08 8372 0999
e-mail: info@hkaustralia.com

New Zealand: Human Kinetics
P.O. Box 80
Torrens Park, South Australia 5062
0800 222 062
e-mail: info@hknewzealand.com

E6309

To the victims of terrorism—all over the world.

CONTENTS

FOREWORD

AT 7:55 ON THE MORNING OF APRIL 15, 2013, I climb up the metal scaffolding that serves as the photo bridge spanning the finish line of the Boston Marathon. Heading to my commentary position in front of WBZ-TV (CBS) cameras, this will be my 36th consecutive telecast of the Boston Marathon, which, as it turns out, is every televised edition of the race. Every race has a story; without fail, as I make my annual walk for the start, those years of the races peel back and spin out a history that amazes me. What will happen today?

As I squeeze behind a makeshift desk high over the finish, I can't help but think of the unlikely beginning that got me here. Of my old coach Arnie who told me every story of his 15 Boston Marathons so often in 1966, my first serious year of running, that I fell in love with the sacred race and asked him to train me for it.

He did train me, and I registered for the 1967 race using my initials, K.V., because that was how I signed my name. Boston was a men-only event then, and race codirector Jock Semple was so infuriated that I was running in his event that he attacked me at the two-mile mark and tried to rip off my bib numbers. My burly boyfriend charged into Jock and sent him out of the race instead. I was scared but very determined, and I went on to finish the race.

The incident radicalized me and other women. We came back to Boston and ran again and again, determined to change the rules. The male runners were totally supportive, but plenty of nonrunners were not. They didn't deter us; we loved running the Boston Marathon more than any hate.

Below me now, the finish line area is beginning to come to life. Three policemen with sniffer dogs are sweeping back and forth across the street. I think how sad it is that we have to have this security, but I am glad for it. In those radicalizing days of the early '70s, I had a lingering nightmare that some weirdo sniper from a rooftop along the finish would take me out for barging into a men's event.

The women prevailed, and it was in the 1972 Boston where we were first officially admitted. Suddenly, the world knew women could run; more important, *women* knew they could run. Two months later, Title IX was passed. A sea change in women's equality and capability began and led to the 1981 acceptance of a women's marathon in the Olympics.

Thinking about my opening remarks for the show, I decide to focus on Shalane Flanagan; at last we had a great American who was a definite contender. As I put my notes together, I keep thinking about another Boston, 1983, when Joan Benoit just trashed the world record with her 2:22:43 run and set herself up as the gold medal contender in Los Angeles. I loved doing that commentary! It was like watching the future unfold.

Still, when I do my opening, I tag it with Kenyan Rita Jeptoo, who I really feel will win. And I thought then of the Kenyan emergence for both men and women. I called Boston in 1988 when Ibrahim Hussein was the first African to win the Boston Marathon and the man who opened the floodgates to the great athletes of the Rift Valley, first male and then female. From there came increasingly stunning performances at Boston, the greatest of which was Geoffrey Mutai's 2:03:02 in 2011, the fastest marathon ever run.

We talk about the weather. It is a perfect day for running—cool and partly sunny. We talk about the significance of having a horn but no gun at the start as a commemoration to the 26 schoolchildren and school staff members who were killed by a deranged gunman in Newtown, Connecticut. We talk about how the race is more than about running. At the finish line, it is Lelisa Desisa from Ethiopia and Rita Jeptoo from Kenya who break the tape.

Soon after the elites finish come the runners who have flattened themselves to get a BQ—a Boston qualifier. These are the people who use Boston as their final or even annual test and to satisfy their need to be their own heroes. They've trained hard. I thought of Dr. George Sheehan, our running guru of the 1970s and '80s, who said something like "If you take it seriously, then every spring, you get yourself up to Boston." To Dr. Sheehan, Boston was a ritual of atonement, and we all agreed.

The street begins to fill, wall to wall. These are the slower runners, sure, but they are running well. Several of them I'd met the day before at the expo and signed their bibs with "Be Fearless!" Many are older age-group qualifiers, and many are charity runners, who had raised enough money to get a starting number in exchange for a contribution. I thought about how running has transformed donating into a cause of the heart and legs, not just of the checkbook, and created a multibillion-dollar industry, something unimagined when I was running.

A lot was unimagined then; many of us had grown up in this race, wondrously going from geeky runners into mainstream event promoters, writers, agents, sport physicians, and running retailers. Our marathon had become huge, rich, and famous, and we were all thrilled by being a part of making it happen and of having it be a big part of our very livelihoods. How good can it get when you make your living from running, the activity you love most?

At 1:30, after five straight hours of commentating, we end our live broadcast. I hug my co-commentator good-bye and head to the official race hotel and media center, where my husband, Roger Robinson, and I are staying. He's still writing in the press center. I go to our room and put down my notebook. My watch, left on race time, says 4:09, and the first bomb goes off. Then the second. Our hotel goes into lockdown, and from my window I watch as color and joy turn into a surreal scene resembling a military coup.

For every person who was in Boston on April 15, 2013, that day has a story. All stories involve parts of this history that has changed us, and they all involve love for an activity that takes us beyond running. Love often brings heartbreak, but never before has such pain produced such determination to prevail and build back stronger. In this book, Hal Higdon, an old friend who grew up in this race like the rest of us, has uniquely captured the immediate movements and words of many runners who were there. Through their instantaneous Internet messages, we hear their stories like never before. Now they, too, create a new chapter in this astonishing history.

—Kathrine "K.V." Switzer

PREFACE

4:09:43 BEGAN ON SOCIAL MEDIA, a "good-luck" wish I offered on Facebook on Sunday afternoon, April 15, 2013, to those preparing for the 117th running of the Boston Athletic Association Marathon. Monday, I brazenly suggested, would be a "perfect day." Perfect, because of cool weather predicted, ideal for securing a PR or another BQ. Several dozen runners, beginning with Neil Gottlieb of Philadelphia, quickly responded with comments.

Neither I nor any of my Facebook friends imagined how less perfect a day April 15, 2013, would be, how two bombs planted near the finish line on Boylston Street by two misguided youths would turn what had begun as a joyous day into a tragic one.

I had no expectations that I might write this book, either on Sunday before the marathon, Monday during the marathon, or for several days after what must be judged as Boston's most historic marathon. I was not in Boston. I was neither running the race nor covering it, as I have often done, for a publication like *Runner's World*. I was 935 miles away at home in Indiana, viewing what happened on the Internet with horror.

For several days after the bombing, I even exchanged emails with a friend and colleague who had run Boston, trying to convince him that *he* should be the one to write the definitive book about the events of April 15. "You owe it to the running world to tell the story of Boston 2013 from the point of view of the runners, *our* point of view," I insisted. I didn't want to trust the inevitable retelling of the day's events to someone with less a knowledge of, or less of a love for, the Boston Marathon.

Alas, my friend and colleague was in the middle of writing another book with a deadline hanging over his head. He also was in the middle of a move into a new house, all the packing and unpacking that required. And perhaps he was still somewhat traumatized by the day's events, the fact that he was still on the course approaching Boylston when the bombs exploded. Sometimes you can be too close. Other sports reporters who might have produced Boston 2013 books (and who still may) were prevented by a police lockdown from venturing out of the Press Room to view the scene of the explosions. Maybe viewing Boston 2013 via the Internet from a distance of 935 miles away was less a problem than I first imagined.

Meanwhile, in the next several days and weeks and eventually stretching into months, those who had been participants in the 2013 Boston Marathon began to offer their stories, not to reporters but to friends and family through the Internet. "Breaking News" no longer appears only on TV and in newspapers. These storytellers had been participants in Boston's most historic marathon. Like TV commentator Kathrine Switzer, who provided the touching foreword to this book, they were there when the bombs went off, and they would remember what they were doing when they heard the explosions, or heard of the explosions. These participants were finished runners back in their hotels, finished runners still working their way through the land of foods and fluids, unfinished runners on Boylston Street who both saw and felt the explosions, and unfinished runners locked from access to what had become a crime scene.

Because I have a large presence in cyberspace, those runners soon began to share their stories with me on Facebook, offering links to their blogs on my page, "Hal Higdon's Marathon." I became a conduit for their first-person stories, many of those stories riveting! As the blog links multiplied, I began to visualize the book you have just finished reading: *4:09:43* would collect these stories (close to 75 of them), organizing them into a single-voiced narrative that would move from Boston Common to the Athletes' Village to Hopkinton Green and through the eight municipalities that make up the Boston course to Boylston Street. I visualized a book that would not merely reprint the stories of 75 runners; it would tell the story as though there were a single, mythical runner with 75 pairs of eyes.

Obviously without the 75 sets of eyes, *4:09:43* could not have been written. I have published more than three dozen books during a long life as author and journalist. Releasing *4:09:43* to the world (not merely the running world), I consider this my best work. Of course, I have thought this previously about many of my books.

What I feel is unique about *4:09:43* is that it may be the first book about a major sporting event researched through social media.

BOSTON MARATHON®
Official JetBlue Course Map

©2013, Boston Athletic Association. All rights reserved.

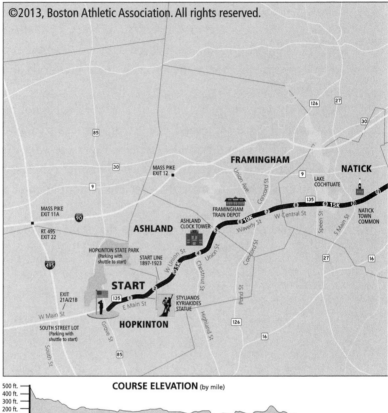

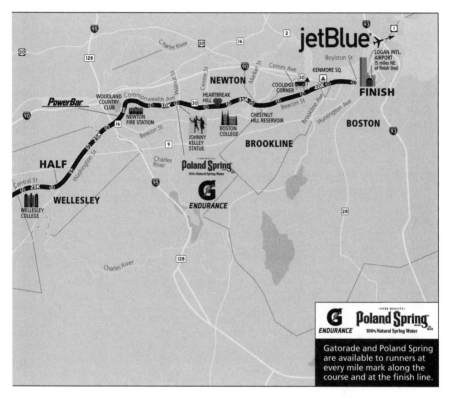

Courtesy of the Boston Athletic Association. Used with permission. B.A.A. © 2013.

INTRODUCTION

ON SUNDAY AFTERNOON, APRIL 14, 2013, many of those planning to participate in the 117th running of the Boston Athletic Association Marathon the following morning had retreated to their hotel rooms after a day of sightseeing with their families. During a visit to the Expo at the Hynes Convention Center, they had picked up the bibs that would on Monday allow them entry into the corrals in suburban Hopkinton, the start point of the world's oldest and most prestigious marathon.

Boston! The great city's name reverberates in the minds of marathoners, possessing a meaning that stretches beyond its historic roots.

Most of those staying in the several dozen hotels conveniently positioned near the finish line on Boylston Street, the Back Bay area, the heart of the city, were not by any stretch of the imagination "elite" athletes. They would not be seen on TV the next morning running with the pack of feather-footed Kenyans and Ethiopians. But they certainly represented a sub-elite: runners who had achieved a BQ, or Boston Qualifying time. They were the Chosen Ones, who had obtained entry into "The Boston" by meeting strict qualifying standards: 3:05 for men between the ages of 18 and 35; 3:35 for women that same age with gradually easier standards for those older in five-year age divisions. (Men over 80 could achieve a BQ by running 4:55; women that age, 5:25.) To have met such standards and be permitted to run Boston gave these runners near celebrity status among their running peers. For the 117th running, the sponsoring Boston Athletic Association had allowed approximately 25,000 qualified runners into its field.

A third group of generally slower athletes were neither elite nor sub-elite, but in many respects their achievements might be considered as great or greater. The B.A.A. had welcomed them into the field for their fundraising efforts. Some 2,000 charity athletes were entered, having raised $16 million for the privilege of joining the elites and sub-elites on the historic 26-mile 385-yard course. Not everybody entered would choose to run. Injuries suffered while training sometimes took a toll. Activities other than running, a cousin's wedding, a business trip, often interfered. A total of 23,000 runners from all groups had picked up their bibs at the three-day Expo on Friday, Saturday, and Sunday. They would run what, unexpectedly, would become Boston's most historic race.

For a time on Sunday afternoon, many of the marathoners nervously stalked the city streets, roamed the aisles of the Expo, or waited in their hotel rooms or in their homes in Boston and its surrounding towns and suburbs.

They included Neil Gottlieb, who had a corner room on the sixth floor of the Fairmont Copley Plaza Hotel, a historic hotel built in 1912, just around the corner from the marathon's finish line. Gottlieb, 44, a senior vice president of sales for 3FX, a medical animation company based in Philadelphia, had just finished lunch with his family at Uno's Pizza on Boylston Street. Seated on a bench in the mall adjacent to the Marathon Expo, sharing a frozen yogurt with his 5-year-old son, he reached for his iPhone and surfed the Internet, landing on my Facebook page. It was mid-afternoon. I was 935 miles away in Indiana, but Boston was on my mind. I decided to offer a shout-out to my friends running the marathon.

"Yo, Facebook Followers: Any of you running Boston tomorrow, maybe hanging out in your room after spending too much time walking around the Expo? Relax. You'll do well. Let us hear from you."

Neil Gottlieb became the first to respond. Tapping his iPhone rapidly with two thumbs, he wrote: "That is exactly what I am doing! Chilling for a bit before the carb-a-thon continues! If you are here, I would love to shake your hand and say hello! Keep missing you at different races around the country this year." Facebook, ever anal with numbers, revealed that Gottlieb offered this response on "April 14 at 2:35 p.m."

Heather Lee-Callaghan posted her comment only two minutes later: "I'm ready for Boston! Followed your Intermediate-2 plan." The reference was to one of the many marathon training programs I offer on the Internet. Hundreds, maybe thousands of runners at Boston this year, had achieved their BQs by following my training plans. I felt a bond with them.

Quickly, the responses popped onto my Facebook page, landing nearly one a minute. Stu Weiner said he was running his second Boston. Lisa Simons Ramone admitted that she was not running Boston, but wished everybody good luck, saying, "Maybe someday I will join you!"

It seemed like everybody responding on Facebook talked with exclamation points. That included Eric Brigham: "Relaxing at the hotel watching some golf tournament in Georgia! Had a nice easy two-mile shake-out run this morning. Got here using your Boston training program!!" Two exclamation points from Eric.

The responses kept tumbling into my niche of cyberspace, Facebook dutifully identifying most of the responses as coming "via mobile." Christy Duffner boasted: "I'm ready and relaxing at the Fairmont! Bring it!" Christy had garnered at least one "like" already for her hubris in challenging the race course. Gina Bartolacci commented that she was content, "knowing the weather will be nothing like last year's!!"

Whitney B. Wickes joined the discussion: "Hey Hal! Sitting in my hotel room doing the usual prerace thing: questioning my last few longs runs, wondering what that little ache I feel in my foot is, contemplating what to wear tomorrow, etc."

Alaine Perling confessed that she was not running the next day, but had come to Boston to cheer a friend, whom she identified only by bib number: 13470. (The friend was Krista L. Wohnrade.)

Kristin Reda Stevens planned to run despite a nagging injury: "Taping up my plantar fasciitis in the a.m. and hoping for the best. Great to be in Boston!"

Great to be in Boston! Those words would come to haunt many of us.

Peg Largo, meanwhile, offered the kind of thanks that any coach would love to hear: "You have no idea how much support you have provided. It's your plan that got me here. Thanks Hal, for making my dream come true."

During the rest of the afternoon and evening and into the next morning, when Neil Gottlieb and my other Facebook friends left their hotel rooms and headed for Hopkinton, 12,028 individuals would "view" my good-luck thread. Ninety-two would click on the thumbs-up icon, signaling that they "liked" what they read. The last person to post to Facebook Sunday night was William Kenneweg: "It's 9:00, and I will get off my feet. Thanks for your advice and posts, Mr. Higdon. Tomorrow will be my first Boston. I'll be surrounded by the goodness of runners from around the planet. So damn excited!!!"

Three exclamation points!!! I was excited for William Kenneweg and the so many others who, whether correctly or not, credited me for their being at Boston for its 117th running.

The next morning, after having checked weather.com, I offered a final, encouraging cheer:

"The weather right now in Hopkinton is 38 degrees, not much wind, dry, going up to 57 by the time all our friends have medals hung around their necks. What everybody anticipating Boston 2013 would call a 'No Excuses' day."

At that moment, several hours before the bombs went off on Boylston Street, none of us watching online had any idea how hollow those words might soon seem. I was proud of the many runners I had trained to run the Boston Marathon. I had no idea that I had thrust them into the heart of a darkest darkness.

1

THE COMMON

THE SUN ROSE IN A CLOUDLESS SKY OVER BOSTON COMMON on Monday at 6:03 a.m., the sun's rays casting dark shadows from surrounding skyscrapers over that patch of green in the center of the big city. A 50-acre park founded in 1634, the Common (as Bostonians most often call the park) is the oldest park in the United States. At sunrise, the temperature in the park was a chilly 38 degrees; by mid-afternoon, it would rise to 57 degrees, perfect for running. At that point, around 3:00 p.m., the Common would be filled with people not connected to or even interested in the marathon: students from MIT, Harvard, Boston University, Boston College, and Wellesley, the couples among them holding hands; senior citizens sitting on benches eating popcorn; people in paddleboats floating on the lagoon in the adjacent Boston Public Gardens; tourists, many of them from foreign countries, some of them having just finished the Freedom Walk, a trek around the central part of the city that showcases many of Boston's historical sites (16 sites in all, a 2.5-mile hike, a 10th of the distance of the marathon).

This was Boston, one of the biggest, and the greatest, towns on earth.

On the southernmost edge of the park, closest to Boylston Street, is the Central Burying Ground with the graves of the artist Gilbert Stuart, the composer William Billings, and Samuel Sprague, an American patriot and a Boston Tea Party participant, who also fought in the Revolutionary War. This day was Patriots' Day, the day on which the historic and iconic Boston Marathon always is run.

Listen my children and you shall hear
Of the midnight ride of Paul Revere,
On the eighteenth of April, in seventy-five
Hardly a man is now alive
Who remembers that famous day and year.

Although William Wadsworth Longfellow would reference April 18 in his famous poem, April 19 was actually the date on which the battles of Lexington and Concord were fought, battles won by the rebel Yankees, partly thanks to Paul Revere's warning. In 1894, Massachusetts Governor Frederic T. Greenhalge proclaimed Patriots' Day as a public holiday. Only 3 states out of 50 celebrate Patriots' Day: Massachusetts, Maine, and Wisconsin. For most of the Boston Marathon's history, the Boston Athletic Association held its race on April 19. In 1969 to provide a long weekend, the Legislature moved Patriots' Day to the third Monday in April, and so the 117th running of the Boston Athletic Association Marathon in 2013 would be on Monday, April 15.

Shortly before noon, when the fastest runners would cross the finish line, and continuing for the next three or four hours, many of the marathoners heading back to their hotels would pass through the Common wrapped in Mylar blankets for warmth, clutching sports drinks, walking stiff-legged, the Frankenstein Walk, the Walk of the Dead, wounded warriors so many of them.

But at sunrise, the battle had not yet been joined. Boston Common was filled with marathoners *before* their triumphs. Dressed in their warmest warm-ups to combat the chill in the early-morning air, they stood stoically in a long line on Tremont Street on the eastern edge of the Common. The line went for blocks beside a row of yellow school buses. The runners moved slowly forward, as did the buses parallel to them. At the end of the block toward Boylston Street on the Common's southernmost edge, a bus would stop. Its door would swing open. Runners would board the bus. The B.A.A. would use 341 school buses acquired from school districts all throughout the Boston area to transport runners to the starting line of the marathon in Hopkinton, west of the city. According to race director Dave McGillivray: "We use a total of 500 buses. The cost of buses each year comes to $150,000."

Standing at the end of the line of runners and buses, supervising the entry of the former into the latter was Peter McCarthy, a race volunteer, one of 7,200 volunteers who serve and service the marathoners. It was McCarthy's job to see that the only people granted entry to the buses were runners, identifiable by bib numbers on the front of their singlets.

And so the Big Day had begun.

———————————

Many of the 23,000 running the Boston Marathon on this memorable day would have tales to tell to their families, to tell to their friends, to tell to each other, to tell to strangers not met. Jack Fleming, director of marketing and communications for the Boston Athletic Association, also would issue credentials to several hundred members of the media covering the marathon. At 6:03 a.m., as runners stirred and made their way to the buses at Boston Common, many of the reporters covering the race still slept, had not yet had their first cups of coffee, had not yet gathered in the Press Room in the Oval Room of the Copley Plaza. They would not do so for several hours more, since the marathon would not begin until 9:00 a.m. for the mobility impaired, 9:17 a.m. for the push-rim wheelchairs, 9:22 a.m. for the handcycle participants,

9:32 a.m. for the elite women, 10:00 a.m. for the elite men. Runners possessing humbler athletic credentials would start behind in three waves, not clearing the starting grid until nearly 11:00 a.m. Seated at long tables arranged in a semicircle, accredited journalists would view the race on two wide-screen TVs, one showing the women's race, one showing the men's race. Afterward, the winners of both races would be brought to the reporters to be interviewed.

But the real reporters of events central to the 117th running would not be those credentialed to the media room, but the 23,000 uncredentialed runners, so many of whom afterward would be inspired to upload their singularly unique stories onto the Internet: blogs already begun when they started training for Boston three or four months before; blogs newly created for the specific purpose of reporting what happened on April 15, 2013. On this day, so much of what the 23,000 felt and experienced was the same as they moved through the eight towns and municipalities whose streets felt the footsteps of the marathon runners, but so much of what the 23,000 experienced also was different, much more different than had been the case in any previous running of this great American marathon race. The reporters both outside the race and inside the race would report these similarities and differences. This would be a day that the world would remember.

Among those uncredentialed reporters was Whitney B. Wickes, 23, operations manager for a chain of salons, Aspen Tan & Beauty, based in Aspen, Colorado. Sitting in her hotel room the previous afternoon, Wickes had been among the first responding to my "good luck" wishes. A week after the marathon, she would upload her story to Facebook, titling it, "A Runner's Perspective." She would be one of nearly 75 runners, who would serve as my "eyes" on the course, whose tales form the background for this book.

Wickes began: "From the Confirmation of Acceptance sent to you in the mail to the point at which you finally cross that finish

line, there is something undeniably majestic about the Boston
Marathon. Much of that aura can be attributed to the regal tradi-
tion it has embedded within the city of Boston, and the immense
spectator support it has received year after year."

George Karaganis, 35, a solutions architect for a large tech-
nology firm in Athens, Greece, titled his continuing blog, "From
Athens to Boston." It would take two weeks before he uploaded
"117th Boston Marathon—The Race Report." His were another
set of eyes. Karaganis was staying at Le Meridien Hotel across the
river in Cambridge with his wife, Marina. He wrote: "The magic
of the day started when I opened the door and left our hotel room.
At the same second, the door across the corridor opened, and out
came another runner. The same happened two doors to the left
and two doors to the right.

"By the time I reached the lift, there were six of us waiting.
When the lift doors opened, it was half-full with people half-
asleep, each with yellow bags over their shoulders. When we
walked out of the hotel, all you could see were people with yellow
bags walking toward where they would catch the buses to Boston."

Aubrey Birzon Blanda, 48, an attorney turned homemaker
from Glen Ridge, New Jersey, had chosen the Park Plaza for
her hotel because it was convenient, only a few blocks from the
Common and the buses. Still another set of eyes. Awakening at
5:00 a.m., Blanda began her usual prerace routine, which included
making breakfast. "I take my toaster with me to all races," she
later would confess. Arriving at the Common two hours later, she
found long lines snaking around the park, but they seemed to be
moving fast. "I'm a chatty person," said Blanda, "so I immediately
fell into conversations with runners around me. We were excited
that the weather looked good. Not too warm. No rain expected.
Everything completely normal." Blanda reported the Common
as being filled with the typical excitement of being part of the

world's premiere marathon: The prerace *angst*. The last-minute dashes to the porta potties before the long bus ride. This was a runner's dream—and a blogger's dream as well.

Among the many bloggers was Mary Gorski, a writer from Milwaukee. Her participation in the 2013 Boston Marathon was a birthday present from her husband, Dave. Gorski wrote: "I've been lucky enough to do a lot of other 'big name' amateur sport events like the Hawaiian Ironman, Western States, Comrades, Badwater, the Birkebeiner cross-country ski race. Turning 50, I told Dave I wanted to go somewhere new. He signed me up for Boston. We figured we would go there once and mark it off our list."

Another Birthday Girl was Erica Greene, a teacher from Germantown, Maryland. Greene would be 30 years old on April 18, three days after the marathon. Titling her blog "The Running Extravaganza," Greene revealed herself as having been born on Marathon Monday in 1983. "Ever since then, my parents called me the 'Marathon Baby.' It only seemed fitting that for my 30th birthday I run the Boston Marathon. Greene did so for a charity, Team Mass Eye and Ear (Massachusetts Eye and Ear Infirmary). Her father suffers from glaucoma and also has hearing problems. Greene fund-raised from December until April, eventually raising $5,471. She boarded the bus at the Common feeling proud and confident: proud of her success fundraising, confident of her running ability, the result of "all those training runs on Sundays." But like almost everyone else on the bus, she felt nervous about what she would encounter on the run from Hopkinton Green to Boylston Street.

Also on the bus was Jen Marr, 49, a stay-at-home mom from Ridgefield, Connecticut. Marr struggled during her final weeks training with a tight iliotibial band, the thick band of fascia that extends from the hip to the knee. Riding the bus out to Hopkinton, Marr worried: "Will my IT band seize up again? Can I run the distance, or will I be forced to walk?" For Marr, the ride on the bus lasted forever, though it took only 45 minutes. She could not get comfortable in a bus usually used to transport students from their homes to their schools.

Heather Lee-Callaghan, 31, who had posted her excitement about being in Boston to Facebook Sunday afternoon, also would blog about the bus ride in "Girls Go Running." An elementary school teacher from Halifax, Nova Scotia, Lee-Callaghan had decided to make some lifestyle changes in the fall of 2008. She started jogging on a gym treadmill, beginning at 20 minutes, gradually increasing the time of each day's workout. That winter she met a man named Matthew Callaghan, who had just finished his first marathon in Miami, Florida.

"How far is a marathon?" Heather asked him.

Oops! Bad opening for a relationship, but love blossomed and soon they married. Matt had qualified for Boston in 2011, but was not running this year because of an Achilles tendon injury. He planned to cheer for his wife in the Newton hills.

While Matt slept, Heather was on a bus headed to the starting line of the Boston Marathon. Demonstrating nationalistic pride, Lee-Callaghan had placed a Canadian flag tattoo on her left cheek. On her forehead she identified herself as, "Boston Marathon Virgin." Rookie nerves now attacked her. Her stomach rumbled. Sitting next to her on the bus was a man from Louisiana, who seemed much calmer.

"First Boston?" he said.

"Yes," she replied.

He smiled.

On another bus, Mary Gorski reported overheard conversations.

"Have you run Big Sur?"

"Those hills!"

"How about Pike's Peak?"

"We had horrible weather the year I ran it."

"Marine Corps?"

"I can't believe it fills up so fast."

Also a first-timer, Gorski tried to absorb information from Boston veterans.

"Save yourself for Heartbreak Hill."

"Oh, Heartbreak Hill is not that bad."

"Just be smart. Like any marathon, don't go out too hard."

"There's nothing worse than dying in the last mile of a marathon."

Similar conversations occurred on each of the 341 buses transporting runners to Hopkinton.

Having her Last Meal on one of those buses was Janeen Bergstrom, 38, a training specialist for the medical device company AbioMed. Before being driven to the bus from her parents' home in Woburn, Massachusetts, Bergstrom had risen at 4:30 a.m. to eat a bowl of cereal. For her bus snack, she packed a chocolate pancake sandwich, complete with syrup, in a Tupperware container.

"I had eaten pancakes before each of my long runs since December," Bergstrom would explain. "Why change?"

Sarah Mutter, 27, a personal trainer from Woodstown, New Jersey, titled her Boston comments, "A Lonely Runner's Experience." Like Jen Marr, she was wounded, having struggled with Achilles tendinitis recently. Still, she felt 2013 might be the only time she could run the Boston Marathon. She planned to soon move overseas with her fiancé, Jeremy Huber, a member of the Air Force. Mutter had postponed until Friday the decision whether or not to compete. "Finally, I told myself, just go to Boston and have some fun. Enjoy the course." Without anyone to accompany her, she drove the five hours from Woodstown to Boston, staying with a friend she knew, who lived only an hour from the starting line.

In the morning, she caught a Massachusetts Bay Transportation Authority train (The T) to the Common, realizing en route that she had forgotten her watch, complicating any pacing plans she might have had. Mutter decided that she would simply "let the winds carry me."

Qualifying for Boston at the 2012 Rock 'n' Roll Marathon in New Orleans, Mutter had run 3:34:15. Given her nagging injury, matching that time seemed impossible, particularly when not wearing a watch. Sarah Mutter downsized her time goal by a half hour, deciding that a 4:10 finishing time might be more appropriate for her fitness level.

2

COPLEY SQUARE

NEIL GOTTLIEB HAD CHOSEN THE FAIRMONT COPLEY PLAZA
HOTEL FOR convenience. The Copley overlooks Copley Square,
named after the 18th century portrait painter John Singleton
Copley. The Square served as the epicenter of marathon activity once runners crossed the finish line. Having completed their
26-mile 385-yard journeys, they would walk (or perhaps more
accurately, shuffle) through and past Copley Square en route to
receiving medals, water, sports drinks, blankets, more drinks and
food, and finally their checked bags, after which they could circle
back to a Family Meeting Area near the Hancock Tower.

Most would not need to detour for treatment into the Medical Tent, also at the Square on Dartmouth Street, but they would
be well treated if they did. Fourteen hundred medical professionals, many of them stationed on the course, protected marathoners, also spectators who sometimes required aid. "The Boston
Marathon features probably the highest one-day concentration of
medical personnel in the world," says Chris Troyanos, a certified
athletic trainer, the medical service coordinator for the 117th running of the Boston Athletic Association Marathon.

The Copley's closeness to this epicenter of postrace activity
would allow Neil Gottlieb a relatively easy walk to his hotel room
after finishing. The location also would prove convenient for his
family positioning themselves as spectators on Boylston ahead of
the finish line. He had come to run; they had come to cheer.

Before going to bed, Gottlieb set his Droid alarm for 4:45 a.m., but he was awake well before that time. "I do not sleep well before big races," Gottlieb admits. He turned off the alarm before it could sound and disturb the sleep of his wife, Kim, and their three children: Brooke, 17; Matthew, 15; and Jacob, 5.

Gottlieb had a corner suite on the sixth floor of the hotel with the massive Medical Tent beneath his window. It was dark, the Square lit by streetlights. He glanced out the window only briefly, then began preparing to go run. From weather forecasts, he knew it would be a great day for running a marathon. An experienced runner and triathlete who had run eight marathons, including a 3:15 at the Philadelphia Marathon, Gottlieb knew the sightseeing for the weekend was over, and it was time to ready himself to race. He donned orange shorts and a dark blue singlet, the bib with number 21833 already pinned to it. He wrapped with orange tape an ankle sprained a month before at the Shamrock Marathon in Virginia Beach and placed Band-Aids over several toes to protect against blisters. He slipped over his head an orange, hooded Adidas sweatshirt identifying him as having run the 2012 Boston Marathon (the shoe company being one of the major sponsors of the race). That plus black Adidas sweatpants. He stuffed black Adidas gloves into side pockets and placed sunglasses and racing shoes in the bag he would carry on the bus to Hopkinton, planning to wear an ordinary pair of training shoes until after his prerace warm-up. "The Athletes' Village can get muddy," Gottlieb says. He would wait until after arriving in Hopkinton before having a final prerace meal: bagel and coffee two hours before the start; banana and a PowerBar 30 minutes before heading to the starting line corrals.

Before leaving the hotel at 6:00 a.m. to walk with Kim to the Common, he woke his children to say goodbye. "They got upset with me once when I failed to do so."

Kim had decided to accompany him to the Common, about a half-mile away from the Copley. The streets were filled with runners heading in the same direction. Gottlieb remembers the walk as being quiet, almost eerie. "Nobody was talking along the walk."

Leaving her husband in the bus line, Kim walked back on Boylston past the finish line to an area just before that line, on the north side of the street, the "left" side of the street as it would be seen by runners in the last 385 yards of their race. This is an area of business establishments: bars, restaurants, a Marathon Sports store, and not one, but two Starbucks coffee shops. Kim Gottlieb stopped at the Starbucks closest to the finish line for a cup of coffee then headed back to the Copley to wake the kids. She arrived back at the hotel at 7:30 a.m. By that time, her husband, Neil, was on a bus halfway to Hopkinton.

———————

While Gottlieb was heading out of town, Elizabeth Bunce, 73, was heading into town from her home in Nelson, New Hampshire. In years past, Bunce had run the marathon five times, four of those times for charity. Her best time was 5:35, but since 2003, she had served the marathoners, working as one of the volunteers, handing blue-and-yellow ribboned medals emblazoned with the B.A.A. unicorn to finished runners, sometimes hanging the medals over the runners' shoulders, sometimes giving them a hug. It was an assignment that Bunce relished. It was her payback time for those years when she had medals hung over her own shoulders. "I love to see the looks on their faces, the smiles and thanks they offer us," she says. "Often they offer a hug or a kiss because I remind them of their grandmother."

Bunce had left her house in Nelson at 5:30 a.m. It was an 80-mile drive into Boston. At 6:00, she stopped to pick up a friend, Barbie Latti, who lived in Hancock. They arrived in Boston around 8:30, time to have a cup of coffee before attending a 9:00 meeting for volunteers at the John Hancock Tower on Clarendon Street, a few blocks east of Copley Square. At the meeting, in addition to being given identification tags and lunch tickets, they would be issued yellow volunteer jackets with Hancock logos on the back, the John Hancock insurance company having been principal sponsor of the marathon for 28 years, since 1986.

It would be a long day for Bunce and the other medal volunteers. They would need to wait until the buses returned from Hopkinton with the runners' bags before setting up the medal tables in the middle of the street around 11:00. That task accomplished, they had time to go to the lunch tent and grab a bite to eat. The winning runners, usually spindly legged Africans, would not cross the finish line until shortly after noon, quickly to be escorted into the Copley for drug testing and media interviews. Bunce would not get to hug them, but soon after that the fastest of the other marathoners would come streaming down Boylston Street. Then the medal volunteers would begin their work, which would continue well into the late afternoon.

Boylston would become a busy street.

3

ATHLETES' VILLAGE

THE YELLOW BUSES WOULD BEGIN ARRIVING AT THE ATHLETES' VILLAGE in Hopkinton soon after sunrise, and they would continue bringing runners to the Village for several hours after that. Many of those blogging about their Boston experiences would recall the bus ride from the Common to the Village as lasting an "hour." The bloggers also remembered having stood in line an "hour" before boarding the buses and waiting in a line another "hour" after arriving to use the porta potties. The wait on the starting grid would consume a final "hour." Of course, there were not that many hours on the schedule, but everything leading up to the 117th running of the Boston Athletic Association Marathon in the mind of participants seemed to be rounded off to that proverbial "hour." Once onto the race course, however, the marathoners' movements would be measured by state-of-the-art timing systems in hundredths of seconds.

The time on the clock over the finish line on Boylston Street showed 0:00:00, but soon it would dance to the rhythm of the runners.

Arriving at the Athletes' Village, runners congratulated themselves for choosing 2013 to run Boston. It was the weather. With the sun rising in a clear sky, temperatures had moved into the 40s by the time runners arrived at the Village. Forecasters predicted highs in the 50s by the time most marathoners made the final turn onto Boylston Street and saw the finish-line clock. Nothing like

2012 with temperatures in the 80s, which caused the B.A.A. to allow those entered a last-minute option to defer their races to 2013. Many had accepted that option rather than challenge the heat.

A perfect day! Runners all over America were looking at weather reports and wishing they were in Boston this Patriots' Day.

Wendy Jaehn, 38, executive director of the Chicago Area Runners Association, had come to Boston with more than 100 runners, many of them having trained under the supervision of CARA coaches. Jaehn had chartered two buses to bring the group to Hopkinton, everybody meeting at 6:00 a.m. in front of the Park Plaza Hotel. She stepped off the bus at 7:00 after arriving at the Athletes' Village. It was as though the weather was something she had ordered last night from room service. Jaehn thought to herself: *Heartbreak, it's payback time!* The previous year at Boston, she had struggled in the near 90-degree heat, particularly on the ascent of the notorious Heartbreak Hill at 20 miles. Now she would gain her revenge. Yes, for Wendy it was, indeed, payback time.

Despite hundreds of porta potties at the Athletes' Village and even more at the starting line at Hopkinton Green, there never can be enough porta potties to allow runners to comfortably relieve themselves before a marathon. John Bingham, author and lecturer, often jokes about coming out of a porta potty after an hour in line and immediately going to the end of another porta potty line, part of a continuing battle with nerves and an unsettled stomach. The true terror of running the Boston Marathon, or any marathon, is not climbing Heartbreak Hill around 20 miles, or continuing the half dozen muscle-pounding miles past that point. It is the wait, the seemingly endless hours before starting that cause the best-trained athletes, even the elites, to inwardly quiver in fear.

Arriving at the Athletes' Village at 7:30 a.m., Rosie Allister headed first for the "portaloos," as she called them. Allister, 33, a veterinary surgeon from Edinburgh, Scotland, could feel the electricity in the air: "There was a party atmosphere already: a nervous party, but a happy one in anticipation of what was to come."

She described everyone in the portaloo lines as chatting. "Boston was the long-held dream that brought us all together."

And so everybody waited at the Athletes' Village, an area of fields and tents, three large ones, beside Hopkinton High School, three-quarters of a mile south of the starting area on Hopkinton Green. Among those marathoners quietly going mad was Kate Johnson, 36, a full-time mom from Lansing, Michigan. Johnson had come to Boston with a group of 19 runners, enrolled in a VIP Boston Experience, provided by Marathon Tours. The travel company chartered a private bus to ease their ride from the Bricco Suites in Boston's North End to Hopkinton. Johnson would post her experiences to a friend's blog, "Through a Running Lens." She described Cheryl Kent running her ninth Boston and Jeanine Steel, who had not started running until age 45 and now, at age 61, was running her 35th marathon, her second Boston. Despite having run two marathons herself (qualifying for Boston with a 3:39:31 at the Bayshore Marathon in Traverse City, Michigan), Johnson felt like a new runner, "excited to be a part of history."

She quoted a friend, Tori Menold: "Miles and miles of training, and it was finally time to enjoy the moment, celebrate the pain."

Mary Gorski noticed what appeared to be military personnel watching from the roof of the high school. "What a shame," she said to a woman next to her. "Even at a marathon, we still need to worry about someone doing something crazy."

The woman laughed and said it made her feel like they were prisoners in the yard, being watched by guards.

Heather Lee-Callaghan described tables of water, coffee, Gatorade, PowerBars, bagels, and basically anything a runner would need on race day. She ate a banana and munched on a dry bagel. "I might as well have been eating a dirty sock. I was pumped for Boston and oblivious to small detail."

A television helicopter hovered overhead. She waved at it, wondering if she could be seen on TV in Nova Scotia. Then she heard the announcement: "Wave 1 runners: Begin loading your bags and making your way to the starting line." Lee-Callaghan began to consider her clothing choices. She removed a pair of arm warmers, deciding it was too warm. She retained a pair of gloves bought at a Dollar Store, planning to discard them on the course. "I do not like cold hands," she says. She threw her bag through the window of one of the buses assigned to transport bags to the finish line and began walking along Grove Street toward Hopkinton Green. Arriving at the Green, she realized that she had left her pace band in the just-checked bag. This would cause her to abandon a carefully crafted plan to run at a pace that would insure a 3:30 finishing time.

Sarah Mutter arrived at the Village three hours before her scheduled 10:20 Wave 2 start. After grabbing a bagel and cup of coffee, she looked around for somewhere to sit. She chose some concrete, but it was cold. Riding on the bus, she had chatted with a runner from Wisconsin, whose name she failed to get. A runner from Las Vegas now sat down near her and they shared a yoga mat. A photographer took their picture. Mutter would neglect to get the Las Vegas runner's name, nor would she get the name of a third woman from Wisconsin with whom she had a long conversation while waiting on the starting grid.

Mutter would say later: "I never got any of these girls' names. I know where they are from. I know their race times. I know where they have run before, and where they qualified for Boston. I know they all had a husband or a boyfriend waiting for them at the finish line. Me? I was doing this solo. I had no idea what I would do after the race, or where I would go. I was just going to finish."

Not everybody running the Boston Marathon waited in the Athletes' Village. Many of those living along Grove Street or elsewhere in Hopkinton opened their doors to athletes they knew or with whom they had some connection.

Amy Zebala, 38, a speech-language pathologist from St. Louis, Missouri, relaxed before the race at "The St. Louis House," owned by a 101-year-old gentleman named Sterling. Every year he and his family open their doors to runners from that city. "It was fantastic," wrote Zebala. "They had bagels and bananas and energy bars, coffee and juice, safety pins, Vaseline, powder. We had the run of the house, including bathrooms. It was very special to spend the prerace minutes with friends from our area."

Kara Zech Thelen, 40, an assistant professor at Cooley Law School in Grand Rapids, Michigan, posted her Boston memories to the school's blog, titling it "My Boston." Thelen wrote: "The Athletes' Village was abuzz with nervous energy. Like the other runners, I gathered with some friends to set up camp on a Mylar blanket, inventorying the critical supplies for our 26.2-mile trek: a jar of Vaseline, water bottles, bananas and peanut butter, extra clothes for the finish and extra energy packaged every way possible—from gels to beans to blocks to bars.

"We were lubed and ready!"

4

HOPKINTON GREEN

"MARATHON RUNNERS SOMETIMES ARE THOUGHT OF AS SELF-ISH," muses John Munro. "It is an individual sport. It involves long hours of solitary activity. Yet marathon runners are part of something bigger. To be a marathoner, you need the other competitors. You need organizers. You need volunteers. You particularly need spectators to make the running of 26.2 miles special."

Munro, 49, an IT manager from Alloa, Scotland, offered that penetrating opinion in a blog titled "Running out of the Comfort Zone." "You become a marathoner when you stand on the start line with the intention of covering 26.2 miles in the very best time you can manage, and by doing so giving the spectators something to cheer for, your fellow competitors someone to race and, having laid yourself bare, you give that volunteer at the end of the finishing chute a feeling of joy, when they put that medal around your neck. They know you have earned it. They know that their hours of standing in the cold is worth it. You, the runner, give them someone to reward."

One of the great appeals of marathon running is that you do share the playing field with the best in your sport. In almost no other sport is this possible. Only a handful of tennis players feel beneath their feet the manicured grass of Wimbledon's Centre Court. Want to play a round at Augusta National Golf Club? You need to be a member of the Club, and until recently, you needed to be male. Play that round the weekend of the Masters? It won't happen. Want to take the field or the court or the ice for the Super Bowl, the World Series, the NBA Finals, the final round of the Stanley Cup? Don't even ask.

But run Boston with the world's marathon elite? You are there, even if starting an hour behind their "there."

———————

By 9:00 a.m., many of those who had gathered in the Athletes' Village began a slow and tortured trek toward the starting line for the 117th running of the Boston Athletic Association Marathon. This Marathon March would continue for an hour or more as the 23,000 runners positioned themselves in preassigned corrals on Route 135, East Main Street, the marathon course.

This included John Munro. The Scot runner had qualified for Boston by running 3:22:22 in the Lochaber Marathon in Fort William, Scotland. That fast a time earned him a position in the second corral of Wave 2. To insure a smooth start for all runners, fast and slow, the B.A.A. divides them into several groups, or waves, determining positions near the front or back by qualifying times. As runners moved into their respective corrals, race director Dave McGillivray nervously stalked the starting line insuring that all his volunteers at the entry gates of the corrals did their jobs, so that runners found their spots on the starting grid without hassle. Having run 138 marathons, including Boston 40 consecutive times, the 58-year-old resident of North Andover, Massachusetts, knew that the last thing runners needed was hassle. He would protect them. He would be their mother. He would see that their nerves were soothed. Happiness this day for Dave McGillivray would be for the marathon to run s-m-o-o-o-t-h-l-y, for the marathoners to flow along Boston's classic course from Hopkinton Green to Boylston Street without anything upsetting their plans. Everybody gets a PR. Everybody gets a BQ, allowing them to return next year for one more go in the Greatest Marathon Show on Earth.

McGillivray had arrived in Hopkinton at 6:15 a.m., having stayed overnight at a hotel in town. At 6:30, he did an interview on WBZ, the CBS channel in Boston that was televising the race. He would do another WBZ interview at 8:13. At about that same time, the elite athletes (men and women) would arrive on special buses to be dropped at the Korean Presbyterian Church next to the starting line. With the church offering a private dressing room and waiting area, elites could prepare themselves mentally as much as physically for their races without having to smile or sign autographs or pose for photographs. They could use less-traveled streets behind the church to warm up, a necessity if you plan to run the first mile in 5 minutes versus 10. Five or ten minutes before their scheduled starts, the elites would move from the church to the area in front of the starting line for a few last-minute strides. In doing so, they passed a cemetery that few would have noticed, their focus being so intent on the race ahead of them.

As the time for the marathon start grew near, McGillivray would follow a preplanned schedule with 146 line items, everything he would do between 5:00 a.m. and 1:00 p.m. On the schedule was the fact that at 8:55, there would be a moment of silence for those massacred at Sandy Hook Elementary School in Newtown, Connecticut, several weeks before. *Click! Click! Click!* Every item on the schedule would happen as planned.

9:00: Mobility impaired start
9:01: State police meeting at starting line
9:11: Dan Clark to sing "America the Beautiful"
9:14: Wheelchair introductions
9:17: Wheelchair start
9:22: Handcycle start
9:25: Elite women escorted to start line
9:29: Introduction of top five women

Among those introduced was Shalane Flanagan, bronze medalist in the 10,000 meters at the 2008 Olympic Games in Beijing, China. Flanagan's mother, Cheryl Bridges, once held the world record in the marathon and her father, Steve Flanagan, had a PR of 2:18:36. Shalane certainly possessed the genetics as well as the credentials, also having placed third at the 2011 World Cross-Country Championships, a notable achievement given the almost total domination of that event by African athletes. Recently, Flanagan had moved upward in distance, placing second at the 2010 New York City Marathon in 2:28:40. It was the highest finish at New York for an American woman in 20 years.

Shalane Flanagan was popular among Boston Marathon aficionados for one more reason: She was a "local girl," having attended Marblehead High School. But this was Shalane's first Boston, and she was shocked at the response she received from spectators lining the course. In an interview with David Willey, editor-in-chief of *Runner's World*, she would remark: "It was phenomenal. It was almost ridiculous. I cannot recall hearing anyone cheering for anyone else. All I heard was 'Flanagan' and 'Marblehead.' It was like my own personal cheering squad." Flanagan told Willey that in all her races before—track, road, cross-country—she never had experienced that level of fan support before.

At 9:32 a.m., the elite women started to the sound of a horn, the horn replacing Boston's traditional starting gun out of deference to the Newtown victims. Flanagan ran with training partner Kara Goucher by her side, but she focused her attention on Kenyan Rita Jeptoo, winner at Boston in 2006. Jeptoo had taken two years off while having a baby, had placed sixth at Boston in 2012, but returned this year as one of the favorites. Flanagan did not plan to challenge Jeptoo or any of the fast Africans this early in the race. Instead, she would tuck in behind the leaders and look for the right spot to make a move. No American, male or female, had won Boston since Lisa (Larsen-Weidenbach) Rainsberger in 1985. Many thought Shalane Flanagan might end this American drought.

The moment Flanagan left the line, she and the other women elites were merely one more item checked off Dave McGillivray's timeline. The elite men would start at 10:00, followed immediately by the others in Wave 1 with approximately 9,000 runners seeded near the front because of their fast qualifying times. Then at 10:20, Wave 2 with 9,000 more runners, and at 10:40, Wave 3 with 9,000 more runners. McGillivray's timeline prophesized that "the last person to cross finish line" would come at 10:50.

That did not include several thousand bandits, unregistered runners, who hovered in the rear behind the corrals. They were not on McGillivray's timeline. By the time the bandits moved onto the course, McGillivray would be long gone, having mounted the back of a motorcycle at 9:58 to be transported to the finish line. As he had done since being appointed technical director in 1988, McGillivray planned to return to Hopkinton later in the afternoon to run the marathon course solo, keeping alive his string of consecutive Boston Marathons run.

―――――――

Among those waiting on the starting grid, few could offer as impressive a running resume as Joe Findaro, 55, an attorney from Vienna, Virginia. Boston 2013 would be Findaro's 15th marathon, his 6th Boston in a row, but his greater goal was to run marathons on all seven continents. So far, he had bagged six continents, the five marathons and continents other than North America being: Dublin, Ireland (Europe); The Canary Islands (Africa); Mumbai, India (Asia); Rio de Janeiro, Brazil (South America); and Sydney,

Australia (Oceania). His seventh continent would be Antarctica in 2016. After that, Findaro knew he would need to chase other running goals.

In any other sport, Findaro might have been considered an outlier, almost a *poseur*. But marathoning allows runners, each one of us, to define our own level of heroics. We can select our goals. We can achieve those goals. It is a terrible cliché to say "everyone is a winner," but it is true. Interestingly (and not every back-of-the-pack runner realizes this), many of the elites who finish far, far in front have great respect for those finishing far, far behind. Runners like Rita and Shalane know that without the masses—the tens of thousands of speed-challenged runners filling the field behind them—their own achievements would be lesser and their paychecks lighter.

Despite his string of consecutive Bostons, Findaro had not planned to run in 2013 until he received an invitation in March to join the Tufts Marathon Team, accompanying his son Mark and Mark's girlfriend, Ana Morales, in the race. Findaro had graduated from Tufts University in 1978. He would join Mark and Ana in Wave 3, Corral 9.

After the marathon, Findaro would write for "Washingtonian Voices" about Boston 2013: "Perfect weather. The best I've ever felt before a marathon, both physically and mentally. We enjoyed the camaraderie of the Tufts team prior to the race, everyone taking photos. Mark, Ana, and I were feeling high as we entered the pens at the start in Hopkinton. We met many international runners, including a buoyant group from Mexico, Ana's home country. Particularly moving was a Polish runner with a prosthetic leg." As a runner, Findaro could not begin to imagine what it must be to lose a leg.

Another runner nervously awaiting the start in Wave 2, Corral 6 was Valerie Petre, 38, from Holland, Michigan. Petre worked as a district representative for Congressman Bill Huizenga of the

U.S. House of Representatives. Politics aside, Petre was looking to break 3:30, which would be both a PR and another BQ for her.

Among those waiting patiently in Wave 3, Corral 6 was Michele Collette Keane, who had run Boston three times while a student at Wellesley College in the early '80s. Keane first had watched the marathon as a 2-year-old by her mother's side. Keane explains: "My mom grew up in Boston and cheering the marathoners was part of her life. And our life. We always watched from downtown Natick. Until the late '70s, there were no real water stops at Boston, so we filled trash barrels with water and offered cups to the runners. I remember cheering Bill Rodgers when I was in junior high, wanting some day to be part of the Boston Marathon."

She got that chance in college, joining the "bandits" at the back of the pack. In Keane's first year as a bandit, she ran accompanied by a friend, a rower. Keane was a swimmer, who ran off-season mainly to maintain weight. "We ran the race on a dare from some fraternity boys from MIT," Keane recalls. "They dropped out at Boston College (20 miles), but we kept going and finished."

In her second year, she ran Boston with classmates who were trying to convince administrators at Wellesley to add cross-country as a competitive sport. "The Boston Marathon was not as big a deal those days," says Keane. "Patriots' Day was a holiday, but some of the girls needed to drop out halfway because they had classes to attend."

Keane does not recall her times the first two years banditing Boston. Her third year as a senior, she finished around 4:30. Several years later she returned to Boston better trained and, working as an engineer, with enough money to pay an entry fee. Without the stresses of schoolwork, she was well qualified, having run 3:18 at the Ocean State Marathon. She set a personal record of 3:03:05 at Boston in 1986, finishing 50th among women entries. Some years she worked as a volunteer, both at the Expo and on the course.

In 2013, age 51, now married and living in Bay Village, Ohio, Keane decided to run Boston partly because her daughter Shannon was a student at Boston University. Shannon and her friends planned to cheer Mom and other marathoners at a point near Kenmore Square, one mile out from the finish line. Keane had advised the BU students to watch from that spot rather than along Boylston Street near the finish, where it was more difficult to spot marathoners because of the crowds lining both sides of the street.

Keane arrived at the Athletes' Village at 9:00, met with friends, took pictures, and departed around 10:00 for the starting line. Her Boston qualifying time had been 3:46, which placed her far back in the field, but overcoming a recent injury, she did not care. She checked into the corral at 10:20, just after the Wave 2 runners began to move. Keane's wait in the starting grid would be short. She did not know it, but Keane was just another item on Dave McGillivray's timeline. Part of the smoothly orchestrated flow. She would cross the line at 10:42, only two minutes after the Wave 3 start. In doing so, she passed over two electronic mats which recognized the bar attached to her bib, recording the exact moment her personal race began. This would permit the exact time it took her to get from Point A to Point B to be recorded electronically, that and her splits along the way in five-kilometer increments to be flashed near instantaneously to anyone around the world who might want to check her progress, or the progress of others in the race. Despite her history of fast marathons, Keane had no specific time goals; she mainly wanted to enjoy the day and hug Shannon at 25 miles, her daughter never before having watched Mom run Boston.

It was projected as a special day for both women: mother and daughter. It would become more than that.

5

ASHLAND

AND SO IT HAD BEGUN: The 117th running of the Boston Athletic Association Marathon.

Rita Jeptoo, Shalane Flanagan, and the other leading women swept through Ashland as though on skateboards: smooth, very smooth, utilizing the early downhills to maximum advantage, but not allowing the momentum from the slope to push them too far ahead of sensible pace. In fact, the lead women were running conservatively, smartly, eyeing each other. They had no friendly "rabbits," pacesetters as used in other marathons, to guarantee fast times. They had no males ahead of and around them to tempt the "girls" into making foolhardy moves that might ill serve them later. They only had each other. So they cruised. Jeptoo passed the 5-K checkpoint in 18:39; Shalane Flanagan, the same time.

Six minutes per mile. Given the downhill cant of the early miles, that was almost jogging for the elite women. They were running with their brains more than their bodies.

Back in Hopkinton, the elite male runners had just begun to position themselves on the starting line, jogging in circles, bursting now and then into a stride or sprint-out to warm their muscles for the steep downhills in the early miles. Among them was Jason Hartmann, 32, a graduate of the University of Oregon and currently living in Boulder, Colorado, fastest among the American entrants. But was he fast enough to challenge the top Africans? Hartmann had placed fourth at Boston the previous year on a feverishly hot day in 2:14:31. He had a PR of 2:11:06, set in the 2010 Chicago Marathon. But the fastest of the Africans had personal records significantly faster. Lelisa Desisa of Ethiopia, 23, had run 2:04:35 three months earlier in the Dubai Marathon. The fastest of the current crop of American runners might have stayed in step with the Kenyans and Ethiopians, but Ryan Hall, Meb Keflezighi, Abdi Abdirahman, and Dathan Ritzenhein, for various reasons had bypassed Boston this year.

"I'm just here to compete," Hartmann blandly told John Powers, a reporter from the *Boston Globe*, at a Friday press conference. "That's all I'm here to do. The race will be what it will be at the end of the day."

Dave McGillivray had much the same attitude. Pacing back and forth in a blocked-off area in front of and to the side of the starting line, the race director ignored Hartmann and the others, his attention more on his crew of volunteers responsible for getting the elites and the others in Wave 1 off the line precisely at 10:00 as scheduled on McGillivray's timeline. Two minutes before that time, the race director climbed onto the back of a motorcycle, also precisely as scheduled. During the early miles, he would track the lead runners and the parade of vehicles accompanying them: one truck carrying a TV camera, another truck carrying photographers, a pickup truck carrying a small number of reporters, since most members of the media watch the race on TV at the Copley Plaza.

For several miles, McGillivray would hover near the elite men, then he would instruct his driver to accelerate and catch the elite women, all the time being aware of police officers blocking side streets so automobiles could not enter the course. Finally, he would surge forward all the way to the finish line on Boylston Street to make sure all his plans were in order. Dave McGillivray expected nothing to interfere with the smooth running of the Boston Marathon this day.

The several miles between Hopkinton and Ashland present a unique challenge for Boston marathoners. The challenge comes from the downhill tilt of these early miles. Boston is a downhill course, dropping from 462 feet above sea level on the starting line to 16 feet above sea level on the final run-in at Boylston Street. Among the steepest areas is the first half-mile, nearly a 150-foot drop in elevation, almost a toboggan slide that can get runners in trouble if they run the slide too fast. As much a problem are the several miles continuing from Hopkinton through Ashland and into Framingham: rolling, but rolling more downhill than uphill. Suddenly, runners find themselves moving way faster than their planned pace, a serious tactical mistake for anyone hopeful of running a time equal to or faster than their BQ, the qualifying time that had gotten them into the 2013 Boston Marathon.

Checking their watches at Ashland, smart runners realize this and throttle back, saving energy for the challenging uphill miles to come later, particularly the four hills that culminate with Heartbreak Hill in Newton. Or maybe they do not recognize their mistake until Framingham. Or maybe Newton, by which time it is too late. They are cooked. The four Newton hills will destroy them. And if not then, the subtle downhill from Cleveland Circle at about 22 miles to Kenmore Square at about 25 miles will pound their quadriceps muscles to mush, making the final 385 yards into the finish line on Boylston Street not happy yards. "If I only had paced myself better," is the cry of defeated runners as they soak in tubs after returning to their hotels.

Among those recognizing the dangers that the Boston course presented was Carissa von Koch. She described the first mile as a crowded mile: "My plan was to start conservatively. I had no desire to weave through the crowds. Passing would have been impossible had I tried anyway. We were packed in tight."

So tight that von Koch failed to spot the sign signifying she had run one mile. Her watch, a Garmin Forerunner 305, beeped to alert her. Glancing at the screen, she was disappointed that the display screen showed a time of 7:58. She had hoped to run between 7:30 and 7:35 for the first half of the race. If her Garmin could be believed, she had lost nearly 30 seconds off her planned pace. More the bother, she had lost it on the steepest downhill of the entire 26.2-mile course! Von Koch quickly realized that, hemmed in by the crowds, she had no choice but to relax and accept the pace dictated by those surrounding her. Days later, when she posted her Boston memories to the Internet, von Koch had rationalized away those lost seconds:

"It's tempting to start the race and go out too fast on the downhill. This is hard on your legs and will come back to haunt you later in the race. I had been advised again and again to start out slow so I played it safe. The next few miles went smoothly. It was still really crowded, but the continued downhills allowed me to hit my paces."

Erica Greene also had been warned about the downhills by her coach Fred Treseler, who had spoken at a Sunday morning breakfast for the charity Team Eye and Ear. Treseler had offered two recommendations for the early miles:

1. Start off slow.
2. Do not let the crowd distract you from your pace.

As the runners surrounding Greene crossed the border between the towns of Hopkinton and Ashland at about two miles, those words of Treseler continued to echo in her ears.

Jen Marr described her thoughts during the first few miles in almost a stream-of-consciousness:

It was a hard race from the start.
Mile 1, a side ache:
Are you kidding me? Now?

I remembered from my training:
Blow it out hard.
Push against your ribs.
Don't think about it.
Blow it out some more.
Soon it was gone.

Heather Lee-Callaghan later would recall the spectators: "There were spectators lined completely on both sides, even in the early miles. We ran past kids with hands reaching out for high fives. I high-fived probably 25 people coasting down the first hill. I felt like a rock star."

Lee-Callaghan ran with an iPod, but did not even turn it on until past five miles. "There was enough music coming from off the course. I must have heard the theme from *Rocky* 20 times." Lee-Callaghan decided that the next time she ran Boston, she would leave her iPod back in the hotel.

She came to the 10-kilometer checkpoint, near the Framingham train depot. Lee-Callaghan knew that friends were tracking her times online, "so every time I saw a chip mat, I ran fast toward it and stomped on the mat." She did not know why. "Not like it would show my status quicker or faster." Her time at the 10-K checkpoint mats was 48:44, putting her far behind Rita Jeptoo and Shalane Flanagan, who had crossed the same mats together in 36:04 and 36:05.

It was approximately 11:12 a.m. when Lee-Callaghan foot-stomped the 10-K mat. At that same time of day, the lead women runners, given their head start, were into the Newton hills, closing on the 30-K mat. The women were in the same race, and yet they were not—but that did not concern Heather Lee-Callaghan. Slapping hands and listening to the music, she was having too much fun.

The hard running for her, and so many others, had not yet begun.

6

FRAMINGHAM

JANEEN BERGSTROM FLOATED past the water stop near the six-mile mark in Framingham and did not stop to drink. It was not part of her plan. Bergstrom had stopped to drink at the water stop four miles back in Ashland. She would drink again at another water stop near the eight-mile mark in Natick. Water only. No sports drink, because that was not part of her plan, not how she refueled during every weekend long run since she had started to train for the 117th running of the Boston Athletic Association Marathon four months before.

Bergstrom's first training run for Boston had been Monday, December 24, 2012, Christmas Eve:

"From that point on, running became my life, and everybody knew it. I have a type A personality, and I took this running very seriously: Physical therapy. Massage. Getting to bed early. Running club meetings. If someone had told me boiling frogs in a cauldron would aid my success, I would have done it."

Instead of boiling frogs, however, Bergstrom went to the fount of nutritional wisdom in the Boston metropolitan area: Nancy Clark, R.D., author of the best-selling *Nancy Clark's Sports Nutrition Guidebook*. As she does with most of her clients, Clark asked Bergstrom about her typical eating patterns: What she usually ate for breakfast, lunch, snacks, dinner. Clark recommended several diet changes that would enhance Bergstrom's energy—such as eating a heartier breakfast, having a turkey sandwich instead of a salad for lunch, adding a "second lunch" to provide energy for the afternoon.

"Janeen needed more fuel during the active part of her day," says Clark, "so she could better fuel up and refuel after her runs." Bergstrom's refueling plan also included snacks every 60 minutes during the marathon. On long runs she carried PowerBars and Gatorade Blocks. For the marathon, she cut a single Power-Bar into two 120-calorie snacks. The Blocks, six of them, came in a sleeve. She cut that in half, making two 100-calorie snacks. She carried them in a small belt around her waist. She was seeded in Wave 3, Corral 9, and it took her a dozen minutes to reach and cross the line at 10:46 a.m. She was shooting for a four-hour marathon. If all went well, she would snack at 11:46 (bar), 12:46 (blocks), 1:46 (bar) with one extra snack (blocks) held in reserve before an anticipated finish at 2:46 p.m. Her job done, there would be a feast of food and drink awaiting her in the land behind the finish line: bananas, bagels, a cornucopia of calories. Nancy Clark also had emphasized the importance of refueling soon after finishing to ensure as rapid a recovery as possible.

"Nancy Clark was my goddess," says Bergstrom. "If she told me to eat something, I followed her advice." Although that did not include boiled frogs.

A half century ago, Framingham was famous—almost infamous—because of a bright, yellow triangular sign in the middle of the road saying, "18 7/8 Miles To Go." Runners shuddered seeing that sign, realizing they had that much farther to go. It was an ugly number, and for many years, Framingham was an ugly town, a factory town, many of the factories shuttered or with broken windows. In the last several decades, Framingham has seen an interesting rebirth, led by Brazilian immigrants, who have helped revitalize the downtown area. Run through Framingham today and you feel like you are in another country.

With a name like von Koch, you would never be mistaken for being Brazilian. Nevertheless, Carissa accepted the accented cheers pouring from spectators along the roadside. She was relieved to reach Framingham, because finally the glut of runners on the road around her had lessened, allowing her to settle into a planned pace. That proved more difficult than expected: "I kept my eyes open for runners around me. I wanted to find someone running near my pace to follow. I never found that person.

"Beyond my pacing concerns, the experience of running Boston was amazing. I kept tearing up, overcome by a surge of emotions. From the start, the crowd support was unlike anything I had experienced before. Each mile I ran, my heart filled more with the support of the crowd."

Even as fast a runner as Shalane Flanagan found herself almost overwhelmed by the crowd. "I almost wish I could go back and run the race again in the back of the pack," Flanagan told David Willey of *Runner's World*. "There were so many phenomenal people out there cheering us on." Someone had chalked cheering notes on the road for Flanagan and her teammate from Oregon, Kara Goucher. Flanagan needed to keep reminding herself not to pay too much attention to Boston the Spectacle versus Boston the World-Class Race. She needed to concentrate fully on her running to stay in step with Rita Jeptoo and the other lead runners. A moment's distraction could cause a gap of a few meters to open. Flanagan was track-savvy enough to know that a gap of a few meters could suddenly become a gap of 10 to 20 meters, and her chances to win the Boston Marathon would be gone.

Joe Findaro, running with the Tufts Marathon Team, continued to pace his son Mark and Mark's girlfriend, Ana Morales. After leaving Framingham, they spotted several Tufts University parents and students, who had come to applaud them. "They greeted us with hugs and cheers," recalls Findaro. "We took a break and ate some of the fruit they offered us."

"Every single house seemed to be celebrating with us," remembers George Karaganis. "Smoke blew across the road from massive barbecues on front lawns. Kids offered high fives, and it was hard to resist despite the energy drain."

Among those having trouble maintaining a steady pace was Patti Labun, 56, a cardiac rehab nurse from Laguna Niguel, California. "I tried to keep my pace at 8:50 for the first half dozen miles to conserve energy and my legs," Labun recalls. "The task proved impossible because of the excitement. At Mile 3, I took out my phone and started calling my kids to force myself to slow down."

Labun's split at 10-K was 53 minutes: way, way, way too fast, she thought. "My butt muscles were screaming in pain. I knew I had screwed up, so decided I was going to slow down and enjoy the Boston experience and not stress out about my finishing time."

Rosie Allister could not believe the support she received during the early miles. "I expected a quiet section, as you often get in races," she says, "but the support was like nothing I had experienced in my 33 previous marathons."

Allister wore her name on her vest (what Scots call singlets). "From the first few hundred meters into the race, every few minutes, someone I did not know would shout, 'Go Rosie!' I had worn the vest at many previous races and had gotten the odd shout of my name, but nothing like this."

Coming through Framingham, a man running near her wondered if she lived in that city, given the level of her support.

Rosie laughed: "I'm from 3,000 miles away, and I only know three people in Boston!"

"Next year I'm changing my name to Rosie," he told her.

Steven Foster, 54, a personal trainer from Chicago, became aware as early as Ashland that someone not far behind him had a motto on his shirt that attracted the cheers of the crowd. "It was funny at first, annoying a bit later, and finally maddening," Foster recalls.

The motto on the individual's shirt was: SEXY PSYCHO.

"We heard 'Go Sexy Psycho' every 10 or 20 yards to the point where it became distracting. I said to several runners nearby that we either need to speed up and leave the runner, or convince him to cover the motto. Eventually, we got separated at a water stop, so I was able to go back to concentrating on my own race."

Only days later, after reviewing in his mind the events of April 15, 2013, would Steven Foster decide that there was absolutely nothing funny about someone, whether sexy or not, being psychotic.

7

NATICK

"WHAT ALWAYS TOUCHES AND INSPIRES ME about Boston are the people who come out year after year," says Amanda Cronin, 33, a teacher from Norwood, Massachusetts. "And year after year, they stand on the sidelines and offer their support and encouragement. They want to scream and clap. They want to call your name. They want to offer you orange slices and gummy bears."

While running, Cronin would often make eye contact with different people to absorb their energy, to see and feel that they were willing her to stay strong and finish well. "Dozens of times while running Boston, I have been brought to tears because I have felt carried along by these strangers. It is an amazing feeling."

The stretch of road between Framingham and Natick is a magic part of the marathon course. Beginning around six miles, the road is flat for three or four miles, the longest flat stretch on the course. The road also widens, allowing runners space to stretch out and find their own paces rather than following the pace of others. And the straightaway allows runners to look far ahead and see thousands of bobbing heads, their companions on the road to glory. Or turn around and look behind to see thousands of runners chasing them.

The 10-mile mark for the marathon is just before the Natick Town Center. Marathoners training for Boston cruise through runs that distance almost without breaking a sweat. For a well-trained marathoner—and that title fits most of the field at Boston—10 miles remains a pleasant distance. No sweat. For those using heart monitors to measure their progress, they are still in the comfort zone—probably 65 to 75 percent of max—as they approach the Town Center. Only as they move farther down the road to encounter the Newton hills and the quad-pounding downhills on the other side of the hills do heart rates rise out of the comfort zone. Only then would the 23,000 participants in the 117th running of the Boston Athletic Association Marathon realize that they have challenged a formidable foe. They will hurt. They will struggle. They will even cry, and those will not be tears of joy.

But not yet: For the time being, Boston marathoners could enjoy their run.

———————

Departing Framingham and crossing into Natick, runners encounter a change of street names that few probably notice. What had been Waverly Street becomes West Central Street, although the highway remains 135. After a slight rise and a curve so gentle they hardly notice it, runners pass Lake Cochituate. In addition to the cheering masses, fishermen can be seen standing by the side of the lake, trying their luck, oblivious to the commotion behind them, the staccato sound of soft-bottomed shoes pounding the pavement not being part of their attention span.

The 15-K checkpoint is beside the lake. Heather Lee-Callaghan foot-stomped another mat in 1:12:35. Far ahead, given their head start, the lead women were closing in on Kenmore Square, one mile to go. By then Rita Jeptoo had opened a 12-second lead on Shalane Flanagan, who had slipped to fourth place. Even with her fast track legs, it seemed unlikely that Shalane could reel Jeptoo in by the time they turned toward the finish line on Boylston Street.

For a brief period of time, at least until the moment Jeptoo crossed the finish line, every runner running the Boston Marathon was on the course together. Every single one of them! The 23,000 runners of Boston 2013 probably covered near 20 miles of road. They filled that road, like a snake slithering toward the sea.

Lee-Callaghan had no time to think about what part of the snake she might be. The Canadian runner was suffering a medical emergency. The top of her right shoe was soaked with blood. A burst blister! This had happened to her once before at the Fredericton Marathon in New Brunswick, Canada. Lee-Callaghan did not like blisters; she did not like blood. She knew she would need to deal with the growing crisis. But how?

Lee-Callaghan decided she had two choices:

1. Be totally stupid and continue, hoping for a PR, obsessing over her Garmin the whole way.

2. Stop at an aid station, bandage up, lose three to five minutes, but finish the race and have fun.

She chose the second option, running into an aid station just past the Natick Common, screaming: "I've got a bloody toe! I need a bandage!"

"Sit down," said the medic, trying to calm her.

Blogging later, the hyphenated runner would describe having a massive panic attack: "I'm taking off my running shoe and bloody sock watching hundreds of runners go by as the clock is ticking during the Boston Marathon!"

While the medic bandaged her toe, she noticed two other men and a woman sitting in the tent, Mylar blankets wrapped around their shoulders. "Neither looked like they intended to get back on the course. They told me I looked strong and wished me luck and said to keep going. I wished them well, thanked the volunteer and ran out of the tent like a bat out of hell."

Thoughts continued to boil within the head of Jen Marr:

Look around:
So many people.
Clapping,
Cheering,
Calling our names.
Kids, so many of them.
So cute.
Holding out licorice, water, jelly beans, oranges, ice,
And best of all, their hands.
"Take it all in," I kept repeating to myself.
High-five the kids.
Wave at the adults.
Thumbs-up to the people holding signs.
We were having fun.

Not everybody was having fun. As it always does, the toughest race on the World Marathon Majors calendar soon would take its toll from runners who might be said to have misbehaved, who perhaps had not trained as hard as planned, who had chosen a too-fast pace, who became overwhelmed by the experience of Boston and forgot that they had come to race.

This included Amy Zebala. "The race was phenomenal. It was a gorgeous day: sunny, with temps in the high 40s to mid-50s. After the congested start, the course opened up. Into Natick, I was 5 to 10 seconds ahead of my planned pace, but I was holding back and felt everything was going well. The crowd was vocal, and the miles flew by.

"At about 10 miles, I began to have some tummy issues." Zebala eventually would need to take a bathroom break, but it cost her only a minute, and she was soon back on pace. Time flies when you're having fun.

Erica Greene found the Boston Marathon to be Amazing and Awesome: "The crowds were awesome. There were so many people. It was amazing, so therefore I was never able to settle into a rhythm, because everything was awesome!

"I was giving high fives, asking people if I was going the right way, and asking Team Girl Scouts, 'Where are Thin Mints?' I was having a ball, but it began affecting my running. I hit a wall at Mile 11."

Mile 11, she said to herself. *Really?*

Aubrey Birzon Blanda ran wearing a bib that had been signed by Kathrine Switzer at the Expo. Switzer had been one of the earliest of women running Boston, and she remained a celebrity and role model among female runners. This was her 36th consecutive year working with the WBZ-TV team. Switzer also had signed Blanda's bib in 2010 and 2011, but Aubrey this year had struggled with hamstring problems during the last several weeks of training. Partly for that reason, she decided to accept the pace set by a man named Allan she had met walking to the starting line.

"Allan set a tough pace, and the hamstring felt good until Mile 10." It was then that Blanda realized the reason the hamstring didn't bother her was because every other muscle, down to her ankles, was shot. "Six miles to go to the Newton hills, and my quads were completely dead.

"I was trashed."

Tracy O'Hara McGuire, 37, a stay-at-home mom from Portland, Oregon, accepted the cheers of fans along the sidelines, feeling like a superstar: "Thousands of fans screaming your name, cheering you on, pushing you past your limits. It's simply magical."

But as McGuire later would admit, coming through Framingham and into Natick, "the wheels began to fall off." Her stomach felt full. Her head felt dizzy. She started to feel nauseous—and she still had more than half the marathon to run. McGuire decided she had been drinking too much water, so she threw away the bottle she had been carrying.

Carissa von Koch struggled as she passed Mile 11 and approached the town of Wellesley. Her stomach was upset, and she needed a bathroom break, but someone was ahead of her in line, so she kept running, then she changed her mind and turned back. Once inside the porta potty, she heard her watch beep into auto pause mode. At that point, she knew she had lost track of her overall time.

"I stepped out of the bathroom feeling defeated. I thought of all my friends who were running the marathon just to soak up the atmosphere. I wanted to join them, but here I was stuck in the middle: not running fast, but not running for fun, either. I thought of everybody back home checking my progress online. They would feel concerned for me when they realized I was not hitting my pace goals."

Von Koch went back to doing the only option left her: Carrying on despite it all, running smart, conserving energy, and taking what the legs would give her that day.

Michele Keane felt a wave of nostalgia hit her as she passed through downtown Natick. She spotted a restaurant, formerly an ice cream spot when she was growing up. And then she saw her mother, Jean Collette, standing there as always, waving, cheering, shouting, "Michele! Michele!" This was their spot. Her mother still lived in their old house. Michele remembered how, when she was a girl, she and Mom would hand cups of water to passing runners. She stopped for a drink that was as much celebratory as refreshing.

Then she kissed Mom and kept running.

Jessica Reed, 37, a registered dietitian from Athens, Ohio, entered Boston with anticipation that could, at best, be described as lukewarm: "After doing Ironman, I didn't think Boston was such a big whoop." The cheers of the crowd changed her mind. Never in any of the triathlons she had run had Reed encountered such crowd support. That plus the signs many of the spectators held.

"You Are Not Almost There!"

"Toenails Are For Wusses!"

"26.2: Because 26.3 Would Be CRAZY!"

John Munro also was amazed by the energy flowing from everyone standing by the side of the road: "These weren't spectators, they were supporters, who screamed their heads off, who waved funny placards, who said something like, 'That isn't sweat, it's *awesome* leaking out.' These were supporters who screamed so loudly at Wellesley College, you could hear them a half-mile before you saw them."

The half-marathon was just past Wellesley College in the town of the same name. The belly of the snake had now reached that point in the Boston Marathon.

8

WELLESLEY

AMONG THE PIONEERS OF WOMEN'S RUNNING is at least one Wellesley College graduate. Her name is Joan Ullyot, M.D., class of 1961, now a resident of Scottsdale, Arizona. Ironically during four years as an undergraduate, Joan never bothered to wander over to the northern edge of campus to watch marathoners pass each Patriots' Day.

"I wasn't an athlete or a runner back then, so I never went out to watch a few dozen men run by in their boxer shorts," she says dismissively.

Dr. Ullyot's attitude changed after graduation from medical school. With the barriers to women athletes crumbling, she started running with the Dolphin South End club founded by Walt Stack in San Francisco. She ran Bay to Breakers when it opened to women in 1971. She ran her first marathon two years later. Ullyot would go on to run Boston 10 times, 3 of those times faster than 3:00, her best 2:54:17 in 1984, when she was the first women's master at Boston, earning her a permanent position on the circular plaque imbedded in the sidewalk at Copley Square. More important to the development of women's running, she wrote a book in 1976 titled exactly that: *Women's Running*. The book would sell more than 300,000 copies in several editions. At the 117th running of the Boston Athletic Association Marathon, women provided 43 percent of the 23,000-runner field.

"Once I did run Boston and passed the Wellesley campus and saw all the women cheering runners, male and female, it brought tears to my eyes," says Dr. Ullyot. "I was thrilled by the cheers. If Wellesley had a cross-country or track team while I was in school, maybe I would have started running earlier."

Another Wellesley alum actually running this year's Boston Marathon was Michele Keane, class of 1983, riding an emotional high from Natick, where she grew up, to Wellesley, where she attended college. Keane's childhood home was only 1.5 miles from the entrance to campus. The spot on the border between Natick and Wellesley where her mother cheered her was only a half-mile from campus. "I always run this section of the course too fast," says Keane. "Way too fast! Even the previous year, with temperatures in the 80s, I ran too fast between Natick and Wellesley. I usually pay the price the second half of the race."

That was a price Keane happily paid. She did not need or expect a lightning fast finishing time. Boston in the spring was for fun; other marathons in the fall were for fast performances. Keane already was planning a fall marathon in Indianapolis, where she could claim another BQ, if necessary. Running past her alma mater, she reveled in the attention paid her and the other runners. "The girls cheering didn't know I had gone to Wellesley," says Keane. "I wasn't wearing anything to identify me as an alum. It didn't matter. They couldn't possibly have cheered louder anyway."

The cheers! The cheers!

Long before runners reached Wellesley College, runners in the 117th running of the Boston Athletic Association Marathon could hear the cheering of women standing beside the road, that part of the course referred to as "The Scream Tunnel." The high-pitched screams of the Wellesley women proved piercing, somewhere between the decibel level of 120 for an ambulance siren to 160 for a jet plane taking off.

"We entered the town limits, and soon I heard their cheers," Mary Gorski would recall. "The noise literally was ear-piercing. Then there were the 'Kiss Me' signs. The students offered to kiss for causes, to kiss men, and sometimes other women, depending on their hair color. *Kiss, kiss, kiss!* It was all in fun and it brought smiles to everybody's faces. That was what the day was supposed to be: All in fun. Celebrating the joy of sport, a commonality that brings together people of all walks of life, all religious and ethnic backgrounds, all political outlooks. Sports is the great leveler. What a person does and how much he or she makes becomes secondary to the shared love of sport."

Among the signs held by Wellesley women, noted Jessica Reed, was one that said: "Stop Running After Your Dreams. I'm Right Here."

Kayla Gaulke, 25, a school counselor from River Falls, Wisconsin, wrote later, "I love running, because you never hear anyone booing." Gaulke would remember the "Kiss Me" signs she saw coming through Wellesley. Girls wanting to be kissed for various funny reasons. She saw two signs saying "Kiss Me, I'm From Minnesota," but none from Wisconsin. Leaving the Wellesley campus, she heard a male runner say, "Oh yeah, I got nine of them this year!"

Heather Lee-Callaghan, blister temporarily treated, shoe bloody but, oh well, had settled into her let's-have-fun mode by the time she entered the Scream Tunnel. She saw Santa. A werewolf. Someone dressed as Queen Elizabeth.

Rosie Allister recalls: "I had read about the Wellesley Scream Tunnel, but nothing prepared me for it. It was like a wall of sound. The signs were hilarious. Two girls were wearing just strapless bikinis and had large signs covering them: 'If You Run Faster, I'll Drop My Sign.' Though running almost at a PB (Personal Best) pace in conditions much warmer than the snow I had trained on in the Scottish hills all winter, it didn't feel like much of an effort. Boston was like one big running party."

Craig Smith, 46, a management trainer from Newcastle upon Tyne in the U.K., warned of the Wellesley scene in his blog, titled "Craig Smith's Marathon Odyssey": "Many a middle-aged male runner has lost vital seconds in the clutches of these kiss-hungry females." Smith, a member of the Heaton Harriers, managed to resist: He passed through 13.1 miles on a pace that would take him close to a 3:00 marathon despite having started in Wave 2. "I was feeling good. My splits were consistent, and I found myself steadily overtaking Wave 1 runners who had started 20 minutes ahead of me." Smith knew that he would encounter the Newton hills in another few miles, but his focus was on the moment, each step bringing him closer to the finish line on Boylston Street.

Aubrey Blanda glanced at her watch as she passed the half-marathon point in a time a full minute faster than in her PR marathon at the B&A Trail Marathon the previous year. (Blanda's BQ time had been 3:53:45, set on her 47th birthday.) *Oops*, she thought. Blanda knew that even with the downhills in the early miles, she had made a serious pacing mistake and would pay for it. Worse, she thought: "I have the entire second half to go!"

She slowed: "I dawdled." As she came to the college kids, she ignored the pulsating rhythm of bongo drums being beaten madly and tried to enjoy the vibes. But she could milk no enjoyment from her race so far. "At that point, I just wanted to finish, and get that medal, and be done with Boston."

Jen Marr felt the same. She could sense trouble brewing as she passed through Wellesley. Her right knee began to ache, the early warning of a simmering IT band injury that had plagued Marr the past few months. She had scouted the course before and knew that there was a water stop near Mile 14, several miles past the college. Her plan had been to stop long enough to fill her water and Gatorade bottles, then not stop after that. Explains Marr: "If you stop on a bad IT band, your leg seizes, and it becomes very painful to start running again."

Alas: As Marr slowed for the water stop, that is exactly what happened. She felt her leg start to seize, so she kept going. *Bad! Bad! Bad!* Marr thought. "I was mad. I was hurt. I was angry." She worried, "How can I do this?" She had gutted through a similar IT band problem for six miles during a training run, and it was awful! Could she suffer that level of pain again? It would be so easy to walk off the course and catch a ride back to Boston some way or another.

Marr pushed such negative thoughts out of her mind: "Okay, I did 6 when hurt; I can do 12." She limped, she hobbled, and before long she was back running. A half-mile down the road, a man popped out of the crowd and offered her a bottle of Gatorade, and it fit in her belt. *Thank you, God!* But Jen Marr knew that the most dreadful part of the course was yet to come only three miles down the road: the Newton hills. It would get ugly!

9

NEWTON

NOTHING COULD HAVE PREPARED Kara Thelen for the crowd support she encountered in Newton, particularly after rounding the corner at the fire station and heading up the first of the four formidable Newton hills. She could almost sense the increase in the crescendo of their cheers.

Rows of spectators five-deep cheered so loudly that it took Kara's breath away. *How long have they been cheering like this?* she wondered. *How long could they keep this up?* "Go, Michigan!" they shouted at a runner just ahead of her wearing a University of Michigan hat. Since she also lived in Michigan, Thelen gratefully embraced the cheers as belonging to her, too. "Go girl with the green shirt and brown ponytail!" That was her. Then after she passed, "Go Kara!" She had written her name with a black Sharpie on the back of a bright yellow pair of Mizuno racing flats, along with the names of her husband, Jim, and children. Also on the shoes was her mantra prayer: *Fast! Strong! Grateful! Blessed!*

"What an emotional wallop," Thelen would blog later. "The cheers were so enthusiastic and emphatic, they took my breath away. And the tears soon followed. I prayed for all the people standing there along the course. And I offered thanks. I was overcome with gratitude for them and their jubilant support. This positive-energy exchange we had struck up was so intimate. For the few moments of my passing, we no longer were total strangers."

Long after her participation in the 117th running of the Boston Athletic Association Marathon, Kara Thelen would still be able to picture many of their faces. "Spectators are a special breed," she remembers. "These spectators were even more special that day."

Shalane Flanagan had experienced the same level of crowd support when she had passed through Newton earlier. Having competed in the World Championships and Olympic Games, Flanagan was used to running on tracks in 80,000-capacity stadiums, but nothing, simply *nothing*, had prepared her for the sensual experience of running the Boston Marathon, where the crowds, despite the best efforts of the police to control them, formed a narrowing corridor threatening to pinch the runners to the point where they would be forced to slow their running, even stop. Or so it seemed sometimes.

Yet the experiences of Flanagan and the other elites was far from being unique among those running Boston this day. In so many ways, Shalane was "just one of the girls," one of the many noise-pampered female runners—and males, too—strung out for miles and miles behind her. The crowds would not discriminate between a 2:26 marathon runner and one on the other side of three hours or four hours or more.

Flanagan discussed crowd noise with David Willey of *Runner's World*. "My ears were ringing," said Flanagan. "I almost wanted to say, 'Okay, this is a bit much. We can tone it down.' The hairs on my arms were standing up. It was almost too loud for me to concentrate, particularly through the Newton hills leading to Boston College. The crowds were on top of you on both sides."

Here was the section of the Boston Marathon course that builds character. Here was where Men were made—and Women, too! A few miles past Wellesley College, the course of the Boston

Marathon descends from 164 feet above sea level at Mile 15 to 53 feet above sea level at Mile 16: a 111-foot drop, a muscle-pounding descent. One big *ouch* for those who failed to prepare for Boston by adding a few downhill repeats to their training. Newton Lower Falls serves as the lowest part of the course thus far run. After that, the climb back to higher numbers begins. All Boston marathoners know about the four Newton hills. They eye the profile maps handed them at the Expo with fear and loathing. They understand that once they turn at the Newton Fire Station after 17.5 miles of relatively comfort-free running, the climb begins, their agonies not ceasing until they crest iconic Heartbreak Hill, it of legends. But before that with runners still within the municipal borders of Wellesley, there is what the late Boston coach Bob Campbell called a "secret hill," a tricky hill, a fifth hill, one that seems not to be part of the landscape or legend. Between Mile 16 and Mile 17, the course does climb 49 feet, not a major bump, but enough of one so that runners encountering it for the first time wonder: *What is this hill doing here? Why didn't they warn me?*

Bob Campbell's hill serves the function of weakening marathoners before their true test. One might compare it to the horsemen sent into the ring to stick banderillas into the neck of the bull to both weaken the animal and make him angry before the arrival of the matador who, red cloak swirling, will claim all the glory: two ears and a tail for behavior most bravado.

After passing Wellesley's town center, Mark Findaro noticed that his father, Joe, subtly but noticeably, had begun to pick up the pace, forcing him and his girlfriend, Ana, out of their comfort zone. Mark politely suggested, "Ummm, Dad, why don't you go ahead?" Joe Findaro nodded in agreement, wished the pair good luck, and began to focus on his own race, not theirs. Over the next several miles as they crossed over the border between Wellesley and Newton, the gap between Joe and the two others gradually grew. "I felt confident," Joe Findaro says, "that without my socializing, I could run the second half faster than the first."

Ah, Joe, such arrogance! Achieving what runners call "negative splits" is no easy task, because Boston's first half is downhill; the second half, more uphill than downhill. After the turn at the fire station, runners climb, climb, climb, climb to 228 feet above sea level by the 21-mile mark. True: Kenya's Cosmas Ndeti ran negative splits in 1993, the first of his three consecutive victories. That year, the Kenyan strolled the first half of the course in 1:05:23, his boyhood friend and training partner, Benson Masya, by his side holding him back. Tom Derderian in his book *Boston Marathon* describes Ndeti wanting to run with the leaders.

"No, no." Masya cautioned him. "Stay back. Stay back."

Ndeti obeyed, but eventually left Masya and covered the second half in 1:04:10 (the final 10-K in 29 minutes), closing faster than anyone before at Boston. With a mile to go, he caught the leader, Lucketz Swartbooi of Namibia and passed almost effortlessly. "He coasted the last half-mile in case anyone wanted to sprint," writes Derderian. Nobody did. Cosmas Ndeti finished in 2:09:33.

But Joe Findaro had not been born at mile-high altitude in Kenya's Great Rift Valley. He had not, as a boy, run barefoot on dirt roads five miles to school in the morning and five miles back home in the afternoon. With the Newton hills ahead, the challenge for matching Ndeti's negative-splits achievement seemed formidable indeed.

When Heather Lee-Callaghan passed the Newton Fire Station, she spotted her husband, Matt, standing beside the road. "I managed to barrel through several runners to hop up and kiss him, say 'love you,' and run off."

Several ladies standing next to Matt started cheering. One shouted: "Kiss and run!"

In retrospect, Lee-Callaghan would decide that the first Newton hill was the hardest of the four. It was partly mental. She feared the hills and worried that she might not get through them without being forced to walk. Many runners using Jeff Galloway as their coach train to walk in set increments: Run 10, Walk 1. Planned walking breaks makes running a marathon easy—so Galloway claims. Unplanned walks, those caused by fatigue, are more a problem. If forced to walk, it may be difficult to resume running. To do so takes discipline, something in short supply in the closing miles of marathons. Nevertheless, Lee-Callaghan resisted the urge to walk, not even a step or two. "I kept chipping away at the hills, relaxing at the top of each hill as the grade started to plateau." One hill, two hills, three hills, four hills until finally she saw the arch stretching overhead: "The Heartbreak Is Over."

Lee-Callaghan remembered wiping tears off her cheeks when she saw that sign: "The course had chewed up my quads during the first half of the race, then destroyed my hamstrings during the climbs, and I still had that bloody toe."

On the other hand, Jen Marr actually found running uphill easier than running downhill, or on the flat stretches. Reason: Less pressure on her IT band. Once over Heartbreak Hill, the course passes Boston College. Both sides of the road were jammed with Boston College students cheering runners, high-fiving runners, offering beer to runners. "Fun at 21," Marr would remember.

Lee-Callaghan would claim later that she probably hit 50 hands on the downside of Heartbreak Hill. She heard someone shout, "You're beautiful!" but was not sure if the compliment was directed at her. She heard someone else shout, "Nice tits!" She knew *that* was not directed at her.

On the hills leading up to Heartbreak, Amy Zebala began to struggle despite the best efforts of spectators to inspire her to achieving athletic immortality. "The crowds were amazing," she recalls. "They were at their most supportive when the course was most challenging." Unfortunately, her stomach still churning, Zebala had been forced to take a second bathroom break. She felt her goal time of 3:35 slipping away, but still believed another BQ of 3:40 to be in the bag.

Nearing 21 miles, Zebala spotted her husband standing beside the road. He did not see her, so she passed him, then came back and tapped him on the shoulder so she could "give him some sass for not paying attention more closely."

Kate Johnson took Boston one timing mat at a time, knowing that friends and family were tracking her progress. The first Newton hill, being a half-mile long, she found the hardest. A sign at the top saying "9.2 Miles To Beer" cheered her up. She remembered her mantra: *The faster you run, the sooner you are done.* She continued to look forward to the timing mats, feeling the cheering continuing at home among those tracking her by computer.

Carissa von Koch also played mind games that involved "miles-to-go." She began to think of her 8-year-old son Lukas waiting at the finish line: *Eight more miles until I see Lukas.* He had been traveling for a week with her mother-in-law, thus von Koch definitely was feeling Lukas-deprived. *Seven more miles until I see my boy.* The anticipation drove her forward.

At 16 miles, Aubrey Blanda felt a muscle cramp in her abdomen, actually a chronic hernia that had nagged at her during the training leading up to the marathon. Blanda waited for the muscles around the hernia to relax, then pushed it back in. "I felt a blister on my left foot. My right big toenail was coming off. Every step at that point felt like a hammer pounding my upper hamstrings."

Still, she thought, "All things considered, it could be worse."

She pushed a mind button to shift from Thoughts Negative to Thoughts Positive. This was her 26th marathon. In 80 percent of them, she had finished between 4:00 and 4:10. She reset 4:10 as her goal.

"I can be happy with a 4:10," Blanda decided.

10

BROOKLINE

"IN RUNNING, THE SIDELINES ARE PART OF THE PLAYING FIELD," Mike Cassidy, an Olympic Trials qualifier, would write in an essay for *Running Times* magazine's online edition. Cassidy's comments appeared several days after the 117th running of the Boston Athletic Association Marathon. "If competitors require us to run faster, crowds inspire it. Nothing can galvanize greatness as much as throngs of screaming fans. Running persists on passion. It rides on emotion. Cheers can't compensate for underprepared hearts or untrained legs, but they can make those hearts beat a little faster and those legs drive a little harder."

Alas, not everyone running Boston could match the performance of Cassidy, who would finish 39th in 2:24:23. Try as they might, driving their legs a little harder proved a near impossible task, particularly in the closing miles. Brookline is the beast, the bad dream that haunts runners long after they cross the finish line at Boylston Street. Brookline: the final municipality before Boston itself. Heartbreak slows them; Brookline destroys them.

The course turns downward after Heartbreak Hill—dropping from 228 feet above sea level at Heartbreak to 16 feet above sea level on Boylston Street. But that descent offers a mixed blessing.

Yes, you can run faster going downhill, but it hurts more—a lot more—and not every runner has mastered the art of efficient downhill running, or is capable of exercising that art when muscles that are drained of energy start to balk. Runners who have taught themselves to run downhill efficiently know they need to tilt forward and land more toward the ball of the foot, converting the foot/ankle joint into a shock absorber. Do this and you minimize muscle damage. But it is not easy. Nobody said it was easy. Thus, if in a weakened state you lean backward and land more on the heels, this is when the real damage occurs. This is what causes the stiff-legged Frankenstein Walk, evident among so many runners as they depart Boston from Logan Airport Monday evening. It is the reason why, for the next week, they will descend stairs backwards rather than forward. Boston is not merely a more difficult course than most major marathons, it is a much more difficult course. It is not because of the Newton hills; it is because of five miles of pounding after those hills.

Tracy McGuire's problem was not merely stiff or tired legs. McGuire had struggled with nausea since Natick. "The sun was warm, causing me to feel hot and thirsty," she would recall. Despite having gotten rid of her bottles earlier in the race, McGuire continued to drink at every water stop. But too much water can be worse than too little water. It made her sick and forced her to pull off the course at an aid station at Mile 16. "Some paramedics asked me a few questions, checked my eyes, and suggested I see the doctor at Mile 17." She walked and jogged another mile, where that doctor took her blood pressure, asked some more questions and informed her that she probably could be developing hypernatremia, a condition where too much fluid intake throws the body's sodium levels out of balance. Simply stated, McGuire was overhydrated from having drunk too much.

"I really want to finish," McGuire pleaded, knowing that her husband, Chris, would be waiting for her at the finish line. The doctor agreed to let her keep running, but warned that she should cease drinking water, only sports drinks.

McGuire nodded. She would have agreed to anything to get back on the course. She wanted to avoid the humiliation of a DNF. She resumed running, but at a much slower pace. "I was trying not to consume water, but it was all I could think about. At Mile 23, she saw a friend and stopped long enough to chat. He offered her some water. She accepted it. "It was good. Moments later it was sloshing around in my belly, but it was worth it at the time."

McGuire continued: "I pressed on knowing I had only three miles left. It was going to be another Boston in the books. I knew I was going to fail to break four hours, but I didn't care. It wasn't pretty, but it was the reality."

Diane DiStefano was having a better race than many of those she passed going up the Newton hills, a much better race. Checking her watch as she came off Heartbreak and starting the descent into Brookline, she figured that she was on pace to break 3:30. *Yes!!!* Best of all, there was her husband, Aaron, and 12-year-old son, Parker, standing by the side of the road cheering her by name. Diane had warned them in advance that she would *not* stop, she would *not* slow, she might wave if she had enough energy to get one arm up in the air. "Don't expect me to be polite," Diane warned Aaron, but he had been to enough marathons with his wife to know that already. Aaron decided to take The T with Parker to Heartbreak anyway. And Diane did offer a semi-obligatory wave and just the hint of a smile before rushing past the pair toward Chestnut Hill Reservoir. She was a woman on a mission. As his mother disappeared from sight, Parker suggested that they jump back on The T and head back to Boylston to see Mom and the other runners finish.

Turning onto Beacon Street with only four more miles to cover, DiStefano was on a roll; most important, she knew she was on a roll. Coming off the downhill, she settled into a steady pace along the long Beacon Street straightaway. She absorbed the cheers of the crowds, but tried not to let them distract her from her mission. She had trained hard. She had trained smart. And because of that, she could enjoy these last five miles more than the runners surrounding her.

DiStefano reminded herself what it had taken to get this far: "The Boston Marathon is the Holy Grail of running. Some people spend years trying to achieve their Boston Qualifying time. Then, once you qualify, you spend months training in cold weather, paying careful attention to do the specific workouts that will help you attack the tough miles that come toward the end of the marathon."

Attack, she would. Diane DiStefano knew she deserved this moment.

George Karaganis hoped that once he reached Beacon Street, he could concentrate on a fast finish. The race for him was almost won—or was it? After a while he looked ahead down Beacon Street and saw the mammoth CITGO sign maliciously guarding Kenmore Square, hovering above the Square, staring down on it. He would have one mile to go after he reached the sign; he had learned that studying the course map. But how far did he need to run to reach the sign? It seemed another 40 kilometers away. Being Greek, Karaganis thought in kilometers, not miles. Regardless how he counted his distances, Karaganis was not there yet, and he knew it.

Are we there yet? No!

"There is a special part of each race that will make your run, or break you into small pieces," says Karaganis. "This point for me arrived around the 36th kilometer (22 miles), when I started feeling weak. The last gel did not get absorbed well and had left an unpleasantly sweet taste in my mouth. I was nowhere near a water stop, so could not grab a drink." After finding water, he did the unthinkable. He moved over to the right side of the road and started walking.

"Come on, George!" shouted someone in the crowd, who had spotted the name on the front of Karaganis's singlet. "Only the straight to go!"

Only the straight! Karaganis kept walking. He looked down Beacon Street and saw again the CITGO sign. It did not seem to be getting any closer.

Examining his watch, Karaganis wondered if he would be able to break four hours. Given the fact that he was walking, that did not seem likely.

Also on Beacon Street, Patti Labun decided that she was both well trained and well paced. Her family would say later that when they saw her at Heartbreak Hill, they were shocked to see her so relaxed and enthusiastic. Nevertheless, with two miles to go, Labun did not quite hit the wall, but she brushed up against it. "The last few miles were hard," she says. "It was the combination of headwind and downhills." A drop in temperature over the final miles is typical at Boston. Once runners crest Heartbreak, they often encounter cooler winds off the ocean. Often, this is the final insult that makes the last miles so difficult. "It got so much colder," Labun would say. She was thankful that she had kept her long-sleeve shirt and long compression pants.

Because of the support of the college kids, Jen Marr had experienced a feeling of euphoria during the descent off Heartbreak, but it would turn ugly, and she knew it would turn ugly. The extra pounding caused shocks of pain, like there were archers shooting arrows at her right knee. *Ping! Ping! Ping! Pain! Pain! Pain!* The arrows hurt. Marr grimaced as she turned onto Beacon Street's long straightaway with The T off to the left. She was going to need to spend the next several miles running parallel to streetcars that she could board and get to the finish line more easily, but without honor. She reverted to basics: the sheer animal act of placing one foot in front of the other.

Okay, I can do this, she told herself at Mile 22, then told herself that again and again as she continued on Beacon. "It was frustrating, painful, and exhilarating, all at the same time. I felt strong except for the pain in my knee."

Mile 23: *Keep running.*

Mile 24: *Just gut it out.*

Mile 25: *I really want to run this last mile at a good pace, but I can't.*

Heather Lee-Callaghan was in no better shape. "The last few kilometers proved most challenging for me," she sighed, recalling the effort it took. "This was where the real race begins and, boy, did I ever know it. Every step hurt. Every crack in the pavement felt like torture. I was hot. I took water and Gatorade at every stop. Drank the Gatorade and poured water over my face, wiping the salt from my cheeks and forehead. My toes hurt—beyond words. My armpits were on fire, they were chafed so badly."

I just wanted to be done!

Like Marr, Lee-Callaghan's number crunching was in overdrive: 22, 23, 24. Only 2.2 more miles. Then she arrived at Kenmore Square, the enormous and notorious CITGO sign ahead, above, then behind her. Lee-Callaghan knew she had only one mile to go—and, there, a mark on the pavement and a sign beside the road confirmed that fact. "I'm pushing, pushing, pushing, pushing, holding back tears, pushing, pushing, pushing, pushing, grunting, but grinning, too."

Aubrey Blanda strode on, her eyes on a 4:10 finish. Except she felt that time slipping away. She looked at her watch when she spotted the "Mile To Go" sign. *How fast do I have to run to break 4:10?* The mathematical answer to that question eluded her. The numbers meant nothing. They did not compute. Blanda decided she would finish when she would finish.

On Sunday, Michele Keane had told her daughter Shannon not to bother going to the finish line. "It's too crowded, way too crowded." Mother and daughter decided on a spot near Kenmore Square, also near Fenway Park, where the Red Sox played baseball. The game was over. The Sox had beaten the Rays 3 to 2. Many of those who had cheered the Sox victory were now standing near Kenmore Square cheering the marathoners. It was a good day to be in Boston. A lot of beer had been drunk that day, though not by the runners. "You can hang out with your college friends," Michele told Shannon. "You'll have a lot more fun. That's what Marathon Monday is all about."

When Michele spotted Shannon in the crowd, she started to walk, then stopped and gave her daughter a hug. "Mom, keep running," Shannon advised. Michele didn't care. Boston today was not about a fast time. She would run another marathon in the fall to achieve one more BQ time that would allow her to return in 2014. She just wanted some Quality Daughter Time, just as she and her own mom had shared Quality Daughter Time years ago handing the runners water in Natick.

"Mom, get going!" Shannon insisted again.

Michele Keane later would estimate that she had wasted only a minute or so stopping to hug and chat with her daughter. The time was well spent.

The Scotsman John Munro was having a bad day. "I didn't have the run I hoped for," he sighed afterward. "I cramped several times. I threw up. I was overheating and could not keep my heart rate low. As I came into the closing miles, I was close to tears with frustration and pain. I was going to run 15 minutes slower than my target, despite the best training of my life and having no alcohol for nine weeks. I ran so hard, but it just wasn't happening, yet over the second half of the course, as my race fell apart, I had to keep trying because the crowds just grew and grew and grew and kept urging me on."

The Scotsman knew that his last-mile agonies were his own fault: "I had pushed just a wee bit too hard."

Among those struggling in the shadow of the CITGO sign was William Greer, except he could not see the sign. Greer was legally blind; nevertheless, he had run six marathons and earned his way into the race with a BQ time of 3:55:14 at the San Francisco Marathon. He had as his guide that day Peter Sagal, host of the National Public Radio show *Wait, Wait...Don't Tell Me*. After the day's events, Sagal would write for runnersworld.com about his experience guiding a blind runner.

"William Greer was really hurting, in that very particular, very painful way known only to Boston Marathon rookies, the hurt that comes from taking the first half too fast and getting hammered by the Newton hills."

Greer kept wanting to walk. He asked: "How far is the 24-mile marker?"

"Just up ahead," said Sagal.

"I'll walk when we get there," Greer replied.

Sagal reported that it was not Greer's best day. Greer, first, had wanted to run 3:45. If not that, at least better his personal record of 3:50:23. Or certainly, run faster than 4:00. But as Sagal noted, "all three goals had slipped away." Approaching the mile-to-go marker, the radio host thought that with a bit of a kick they might still slide under 4:10. He decided not to share that information with Greer yet.

Jim Thelen used public transportation to see his wife, Kara, in several places along the marathon course. Taking the commuter train from the Back Bay station, he got off in Wellesley right next to the half-marathon point, saw her, then jumped back on the train to see her again at the Yawkey station near Fenway Park. Jim suspected that Kara would run the last mile faster than he could cover the distance, even by fast subway train. He decided to skip the finish line where he knew she would be doing what marathoners do after crossing the line: grab medals, drinks, food, Mylar blankets, and their checked bags. Riding past the Hynes and Copley stations, Jim got off at the Arlington station at the end of Boylston Street so he could meet Kara in the Family Meeting Area. He was using the B.A.A.'s SmartPhone app to track her times to find out when she finished.

"The only problem," Jim Thelen realized, "was that my cell phone battery was down under 10 percent, because of the near-constant data stream I had demanded from it." He was not the only person both inside and outside the race to have that problem.

Amanda Cancellieri ran the Boston Marathon even though her grandfather had died only a week before. "He was 84," she said. "Papa had lived a long life, but he had faded fast the last couple of weeks before he died." He had been proud that his granddaughter had qualified for and was running Boston. "You're going to run, and you'll do your best," he told her in one of their last conversations. "Your best is good enough for me."

And in the closing miles of the biggest race of her life, Cancellieri was torn by conflicting emotions. She was happy to be running in this, the world's greatest marathon race, but she was sad that she had lost her grandfather, her biggest supporter. She carried one of his handkerchiefs with her in the race. She was sad that she would not be able to pick up her cell phone after crossing the finish line and tell him her finishing time. The time would have meant little to him. "Papa would have been happy that I just finished."

And so she vowed to do just that. She would just finish.

Finish: Even if you run a slower than expected time, you succeed in any marathon when you finish. You may care how fast you run in hundredths of seconds, but most of your friends and family don't know the difference between a two-hour time and a three-, four-, five-, or even six-hour time. Finish: That's the goal. Just finish. Cancellieri had it right.

11

BOYLSTON STREET

A POPULAR SHIRT SOLD AT THE EXPO pretended to offer directions to those running Boston: "Right on Hereford. Left on Boylston."

Those are words guaranteed to mystify mere mortals: those who have not run in the footsteps of the gods on the course linking Hopkinton Green with Boylston Street. Runners, at least those familiar with the legends surrounding the Boston Marathon, recognize immediately the shirt's meaning. The Hereford/Boylston shirt references the two final turns made by runners in the last mile of the Boston Marathon. Having made those final two turns, runners finally can see far in the distance the photo bridge over the finish line. Still, that may not yet offer sufficient motivation to shift into sprint mode. That usually does not occur until they spot the road marker signifying they have reached Mile 26. Regardless of their mathematical skills, without needing to access the calculator on iPhones being carried, runners know they have 385 yards to run, and they will have completed their Grand Adventure.

Only 385 yards to run!

Are we there yet?

Yes, we are there.

Even the most fatigued, the most foot weary, the most despondent, those who seemingly have drained the last grams of glycogen from their tortured muscles, suddenly discover that there will be a tomorrow. They realize that with a concentrated effort, they can summon the will to go faster, somewhat faster, or at least offer the appearance of running somewhat faster.

After turning the last corner, they find that they now can switch from stagger to swagger.

In fact, they feel *compelled* to make that switch so as not to disappoint the spectators, their fans, their supporters, their loved ones, standing on both sides of Boylston, left and right, north and south. To do less is to dishonor these thousands of mostly strangers crammed into an area about a half-mile long, the final straightaway: the avenue of truth, the boulevard of boasts, the corridor of cameras. *Smile for the cameras? Yes, we will. Only 385 yards to go? I can do it! And I will run that distance with a smile on my face. Three, two, one: Smile!*

It hurts so bad, but it feels so g-o-o-o-o-o-d!

For a moment in time—actually for several hours starting around noon when the first wheelchair racers and then the elite women cross the blue-and-yellow finish line in front of the Boston Public Library, and continuing for one, two, three hours more as the masses of marathoners reach that same line—Boylston Street becomes Cell-Phone-Camera Central, an iPhone commercial. Even though a dozen or more professional photographers hover on the photo bridge immediately behind and above the finish line, hundreds of amateur photographers position themselves on both sides of Boylston, left and right, north and south, pointing their hand-held phone cameras at the heroes of the day passing. It would be impossible to say how many photographs both amateurs and professionals would take this day. *Click! Click! Click!* Thousands of photographs. *Click! Click! Click!* Tens of thousands of photographs. *Click! Click! Click!* Maybe hundreds of thousands of photographs. Suffice it to say, the finish line of the Boston

Marathon would be the most photographed location in the world for several hours on April 15, 2013.

One well-photographed hero of the day was Neil Gottlieb, the individual who had been first to respond on Facebook to my Sunday-afternoon good wishes. Moving from Sunday to Monday, Gottlieb had slipped from a heralded 1st on Facebook to 12,026th overall in the marathon, 8,213th among men, 1,459th in the 40 to 44 age-group. Oh my: That's quite a slip, Neil. Disappointed? One would never think so from the photo eventually posted several days later on Facebook, a photo taken by his daughter Brooke about a minute or so before he would finish in 3:42:47.

It is a shameless display of emotion, when you consider that Neil Gottlieb finished more than a half hour behind the fastest of the fast runners that day. But here Neil is in a moment of unrestrained glory, dressed in red shorts, blue singlet, wearing blue sunglasses, his race number (21833) proudly displayed on his singlet, and he is looking at his daughter, right arm raised in triumph, mouth wide open as he emits a primal scream. This is not the face and gesture of a man who is about to finish in 12,026th place; this is the face and gesture of a gladiator, who, though bloodied, has just beaten his sworded opponent in the day's main sporting arena. This is the face and gesture of a man in the full flight of victory!

There are three other runners in the picture with Gottlieb. Closest to him on the right side of the street, someone who Gottlieb apparently has just passed, is a male runner also wearing a blue singlet. Toward the middle of the street is a runner wearing a lime shirt and matching cap, looking comfortable. On the far side of the street, the left side, is a woman wearing a bright pink outfit. She appears to be walking.

Perhaps 30 or 40 spectators separated from the runners by barricades appear in the picture, too, standing in front of a Verizon store, not too far from a restaurant called the Forum. Some of the spectators are cheering, some are not, simply enjoying the spectacle on a sunny Boston afternoon. Look closely into the crowd to the right. Is that someone in the back wearing a black cap? Look now to the left in front of a Travelex store. Is that someone wearing a white cap? Would either of those individuals be wearing backpacks? No: It is easy to imagine sights unseen. A single cell-phone shot tells a single story, and there would be many more stories to tell at the 117th running of the Boston Athletic Association Marathon this day.

Neil Gottlieb continued running toward the finish line. But the second he crossed under the electronic clock displaying his time, Gottlieb became a forgotten man, no longer in a position to be cheered, yesterday's news, at least among the thousands of spectators clustered around the line, just another sweaty guy walking stiff-legged through the finishing chute with dozens and hundreds and thousands of runners still to follow across the line with performances that, measured against their own levels of abilities, would rate as Good or Bad or Somewhere-in-Between. The marathon is over; long live the marathon.

Stephen Mazurkiewicz finished well ahead of Gottlieb in 3:07:32, then spent most of the next half hour, wrapped in a Mylar blanket, seeking food, water, and a finisher's medal, finally retrieving his checked bag. En route to the Family Meeting Area, he called his wife, Judith, who goes by the name of J.J. She had cheered him earlier at Boston College, but was still en route to meet him. "After J.J. arrived," said Mazurkiewicz, "I put on my warm-up clothes, posed for some pictures, then we started walking toward the Metro to return to our hotel." Despite his fast finish, maybe because of his fast finish, Mazurkiewicz now found walking to be less than enjoyable. "Let's grab a cab," suggested J.J. He did not resist.

Whitney Wickes, another runner who had posted to Facebook on Sunday afternoon, had encountered magic on Boylston Street. Wickes finished in 3:16:17 and credited the support of the crowd: "For us runners, it is such a privilege to have fans on the sidelines cheering us on: people who stand on the course for hours yelling our numbers and names, offering words of encouragement to someone they will never meet. Their love and support constantly puts a smile on our faces and keeps us believing in ourselves through their faith. They expect nothing in return, but they offer us a most unforgettable experience."

Boylston is the happy street for runners. It is our Field of Dreams. Heather Lee-Callaghan was among those who felt swamped by emotions as she approached the end of her long day, en route to a 3:37:32 finish: "I turn a corner, then another, and there it is: Boylston Street! The finish line remains an eternity away. Push. Push. Push. I shift the sunglasses onto the top of my head, so I can see and be seen. Arms waving in the air. Screaming. Smiling at the cameras. I did it! This is Marathon Bliss. I step on the first chip mat, walk across the second and break down, sobbing cries from the pain. Limping. Searching for water. Crying. So happy for my hard work and sense of accomplishments. I felt like a warrior.

"Who knew," Lee-Callaghan would add, "that moments later, I would feel as small and vulnerable as an ant."

Lee-Callaghan decided to head to the Medical Tent to have a podiatrist look at her blisters, the bloody mess that was her right shoe, and the toenail that (ugh!) she just knew she would lose. The blisters on her left foot had not yet popped, but they needed treatment, too. And as she sought treatment, the digital clock over the finish line continued to click down hours, minutes, seconds.

The clock showed 3:53:55 when Sarah Mutter ran beneath it and continued, now walking, into the land behind the finish line. "When you finish," Mutter would blog later, "there are tons of people handing out water, bananas, PowerBars, Gatorade, then finally medals. After being shuffled through the large crowd of runners, you walk over to the buses, find one with your number, stand in line and wait to retrieve your bag." After doing so, Mutter started walking back on the sidewalk on the north side of the street, past the finish line. Checking her cell phone, she realized that she had less than 10 percent battery power left, worrisome if she expected to contact friends and family. Mutter spotted a Starbucks and decided to go in, not for coffee but to find a plug where she could recharge her phone. The coffee shop was jammed. Another Starbucks was farther up the street along Boylston. Maybe it would be less crowded.

Many photos would be taken by spectators, even more than by professional photographers, of the area between the two Starbucks and the finish line. Among the many photos posted on the Internet of runners on Boylston Street, one has particular meaning. It is of Lisa Strong, 43, from Grayslake, Illinois. She is in full stride aimed at a 4:00:21 finish. But it is not the runner who is the most revealing part of the photo. It is someone in the crowd, a young man, college age. He is wearing a cap. And, yes, this is a real individual, not the imaginary one appearing in the Neil Gottlieb photo described earlier. It is impossible to tell from that photo with Lisa Strong in the foreground, but the young man with a cap does not seem to be wearing the backpack that would be seen by various surveillance cameras, including one on the roof corner of Lord & Taylor on the south side of Boylston Street.

By the time Strong finished, Elizabeth Bunce and the 40 or so other medal-hanging volunteers had been working for nearly four hours. Bunce had arrived at her post around 12:15 p.m. She and her fellow volunteers stood beside tables with boxes of finisher medals. It was their job to reward finishing runners, sometimes handing them their medals, sometimes hanging medals around their necks, sometimes offering a hug or a kiss on the cheek. Bunce loved doing this, having volunteered for the medal-hanger job for ten consecutive years.

"The runners treat us like angels," says Bunce. Less so, the unpaid runners (bandits), who offer stories why they too should be awarded medals. "They have mothers dying of cancer, sick fathers, sick children, too. Or more often, 'I lost my number.' We show the bandits no mercy, and that is what the B.A.A. expects us to do."

For the B.A.A.'s race director Dave McGillivray, all the hard work of planning and execution, a year's work, was nearly done: three-quarters of the field now having crossed the finish line, another quarter of the runners, perhaps 5,000, still out on the course, still streaming toward the line, still on their personal appointments on Boylston Street, certain to finish, and if not, medical personnel scattered along the course would be there to help them with rides to the finish line or, in extreme cases, with rides to hospitals. Medical Service Coordinator Chris Troyanos coordinated that effort, supervising his team as they treated wounded warriors. Troyanos had four ambulances stationed beside the Medical Tent on Dartmouth Street, another ambulance in another location across Boylston, for quick deployment and 20 or 30 ambulances scattered along the course or on call.

As runners migrated toward Boylston Street, many of medical personnel and the ambulances would migrate with them on side streets, ever watchful, ever ready to offer assistance to runners in distress. But the day was mild, temperatures in the mid-50s, unlike the previous year with temperatures in the high 80s, when the sirens of ambulances carrying overheated runners to hospitals filled the air. Ambulance sirens are a necessary but annoying nuisance around the finish lines of marathons. Finished runners always try to ignore the whine of sirens, because they seem a symbol of death. With three-quarters of the field finished, Dave McGillivray felt relieved that he had been forced to listen to only a few sirens so far this day.

Now, finally, his work as race director was nearly done. Now McGillivray could play. Play for the race director was returning to the starting line of the marathon in Hopkinton, then running his own personal marathon. When hired in 1988 by the B.A.A. as technical director, McGillivray had run the race for 15 consecutive years, beginning at age 18. He hated to end the streak, but a job working for the world's most prestigious marathon was not to be turned down. Guy Morse was then the race director. Morse agreed that after seeing most of the runners across the line, McGillivray could return to Hopkinton for a late start, keeping his streak alive. And so he had continued to do so.

Heading into the 2013 marathon, McGillivray now had completed 40 consecutive marathons. Only three other runners had slightly longer streaks, but McGillivray was younger and presumably some year might catch and pass them, even challenge the 58 (nonconsecutive) Bostons run by the legendary John A. Kelley.

In 2001, Guy Morse moved up to become executive director, McGillivray becoming race director. Guy Morse retired in 2011, and Tom Grilk replaced him as executive director. Early afternoon, McGillivray texted Grilk to request permission to leave. Nobody in the Boston Marathon field ever has to worry about finishing last. That dubious honor each year goes to Dave McGillivray. He would return with several friends to Hopkinton and retrace the road run by 23,000 ahead of him. McGillivray estimated that it would take him four and a half hours to complete his solo run. He would arrive back at Boylston Street around 7:30. By that time, those preceding him would long have crossed the line, the spectators would long have departed. Boylston Street, except for the grandstands and superstructures and tents and tables, would be back to post-Patriots' Day business. Busy, but not frantically so.

McGillivray's cell phone pinged. It was a text message back from Grilk. "Beat it!" said the executive director.

The race director climbed into his car and told his driver, Ron Kramer, to head to Hopkinton.

As Dave McGillivray departed, the digital clock above the finish line continued to click off the time in hours, minutes, and seconds as runner after runner crossed the line. Originally started at 9:17 a.m. to coordinate with the wheelchair race, the clock had been reset to the elite women at 9:32; the elite men (Wave 1) at 10:00; Wave 2 at 10:20; then finally for the runners in Wave 3, the last to start at 10:40. On Boylston Street, it was close to 2:50 p.m. real time as runners continued to stream across the line. By then, McGillivray almost had reached Hopkinton. In his absence, the finish line clock kept clicking, second by second by second:

4:09:40.

4:09:41.

4:09:42.

4:09:43!

And that is when the first bomb exploded.

12

4:09:43

THOOM!!!

The first bomb exploding was loud, unbelievably loud, unbearably loud, piercingly loud. Rock concerts, fireworks, gunfire, dragster racing, space shuttle launches: All produce noise levels approaching 150 decibels. The explosion on the north side of Boylston Street most certainly was near that level. That is loud enough to cause serious ear damage, even to pierce eardrums. Several runners unlucky enough to be near the first explosion realized several weeks later that they still could not hear out of their left ears. They were not bleeding, they had not been struck by shrapnel, they were not among the count of "victims," but they were among the injured, even though they failed to realize that fact at the time.

A wide-angle image published several days later in the *New York Times* captured the moment of horror. The image came not from a photograph, but from the WBZ-TV broadcast of the race. Several dozen finishing runners appear in the image. A diligent researcher at the *Times* dutifully recorded many of their names, tagging them for online viewers: Vivian Adkins. Hillary Anderson. Alan Hagyard. Joe Curcio. Demi Clark. Those are just a few, and none of them yet have reacted to the horror. Tracy McGuire is in the photo just in front of Adkins, although the *Times* failed to tag her. A yellow explosion behind the barricades, behind the row of flags beside the course, behind the spectators. The cloud of smoke had not yet started to rise over the heads of those who would be critically hurt. The time on the finish line clock shows 4:09:43, indelibly setting that time in the minds of all runners, not merely those shown in the picture, not merely those who had finished, not merely the 23,000 who started Boston that day, but every runner, you, all of you, every one of you, everybody reading this book.

The horror! The horror!

4:09:43.

And 13 seconds after that:

THOOM!!!

The second bomb exploded with a noise as piercing as the first. Because the explosion was farther down the course, away from the mass of photographers hovering over the finish line, it was not recorded as readily by the *Times* and other news sources. On CNN and other channels that over the next several weeks would play and replay and replay the images of horror surrounding 4:09:43, the second explosion appears only as a cloud of smoke in the distance.

But it was no less real.

And the sport of running never again would be the same.

Many Americans of varying ages can remember precisely what happened at momentous moments in their lives: where they were, what they were doing, what people around them did or said. These were moments when their lives, or the lives of people all through the world, changed. December 7, 1941: when the Japanese bombed Pearl Harbor. November 22, 1963: when Lee Harvey Oswald assassinated President John F. Kennedy. January 28, 1986: when the space shuttle Challenger carrying Teacher-in-Space Christa McAuliffe exploded. September 11, 2001: when planes crashed into the World Trade Center taking both towers down and killing 3,000 people.

And now, April 15, 2013.

Each of 23,000 runners at the 117th running of the Boston Athletic Association Marathon would remember not merely when they heard the news, but for many of them when they heard the explosions. And those closest to the blast: when they felt the explosions. They were there.

THOOM!!!

4:09:43.

They were there.

The runners. The marathoners. Those back in their hotels or those making their way to the bag collection area or those still on the course. They were there. Vivian Adkins and the others in The *New York Times* photo of 4:09:43. They were there!

Several hundred had turned right on Hereford then turned left on Boylston and were on the final straightaway with the finish line clock in view. And it happened.

4:09:43.

And they were there.

Though struggling physically, the runners on Boylston were enjoying what should have been a moment of triumph after 18 or more weeks of training. Maybe 1,000 more had crossed the finish line, but were still clearing the area immediately behind the line, where they got a Mylar blanket to wrap around their shoulders, where they grabbed some food and drink, where they received their finisher's medal from Elizabeth Bunce or one of the other volunteers, where they reclaimed their bags from the buses. A few wounded ones with problems varying from blisters to dehydration had stopped or had been pushed in wheelchairs into the Medical Tent for treatment of innocuous injuries, what after 4:09:43 would become trivial. The Canadian: Heather Lee-Callaghan. The Scotsman: John Munro. Approximately 5,000 runners remained on the course, the body of the snake whose head had just been decapitated, strung out along Commonwealth

Avenue even as far back as the Newton hills. Suddenly, their race was over, and they had not run their assigned 26 miles 385 yards.

4:09:43.

THOOM!!!

13

THE HORROR!

APPROACHING THE FINISH LINE, Tracy McGuire directed her attention toward the grandstands to the right, in front of the Boston Public Library, seats reserved for VIPs, friends of the B.A.A. She knew Chris, her husband, would be seated there. He worked for Adidas, one of the major sponsors, thus had entry to that area.

"Chris saw me, but I did not see him," Tracy McGuire would write later. What she did see—and feel—was the explosion of a bomb on the left side of Boylston Street.

It was 4:09:43.

Hers was one of the more remarkable stories posted to Facebook in the days and weeks following April 15, 2013: "I stopped dead in my tracks. I was not confused. I was not disoriented. I was nearly deaf from the explosion, but I knew immediately that it was a bomb. The other runners around me seemed not to understand. They didn't know whether it was a celebratory cannon, or fireworks, or what. They kept running. I had no doubt what I saw, and it was bad, very bad. One minute I had been looking at hundreds of people along the finishing stretch, on both sides of the street, left and right. And suddenly the people on the left were blown up, right before my eyes. Would they emerge from the rising cloud of smoke unharmed? No, they would not."

McGuire's instincts took over. She immediately turned and began running backward on the course, what she hoped and expected would be away from harm. But, no: "Suddenly another bomb went off in front of me. I thought to myself, wait, I was just there. I had just slapped the hands of those people. Chaos ensued, with people screaming, crying, frantic people everywhere."

At this point Chris McGuire lost track of his wife. People seated around him in the grandstands rose as one, fearful that the next explosion might envelop them in its evil arms. They scrambled for the exits. In fact, reports soon would circulate on TV and online (part of the fog of war) that as many as a half dozen bombs had been planted under the grandstands. Those reports would prove untrue, but the sensible thing for anyone located near the marathon finish line was to *get the hell away as fast as possible!* If stunned runners and spectators could not immediately figure it out, the police began shouting for them to do just that.

Dr. George Sheehan, who for so many years served the Boston Marathon as its philosopher figure, often joked that as a skinny runner, he was more suited for "flight rather than fight." There was nothing funny about Sheehan's option now. Tracy McGuire very definitely had chosen the flight mode: "I took off to the other side of the street, hurdled a couple of barricades, jumped over a garbage can, and bolted for survival. I was moving like Usain Bolt, and this was after 26.198 miles. At any moment, I expected more bombs to explode all around me."

Fleeing, Tracy negotiated with God. Since she expected more bombs to explode, she prayed that He either let her or Chris survive. "I didn't care which one of us it was, and actually preferred that it be my husband, for the sake of our kids. I prepared to die, and actually was at peace with it." However, that did not stop Tracy from trying to save herself. She started to run again, through a restaurant, through the kitchen, out a back door. Her instinct was to get as far away from Boylston Street as quickly as possible before another bomb exploded. She screamed for people to evacuate, but many did not believe her and told her to calm down. "I wanted to tell them I had just seen people get blown up before my very eyes, but a handful of people still were celebrating at the bar!"

She continued running away from the carnage and encountered a mother and two small children, a girl and a boy around 5 or 7, the same ages as her own two children. The children were screaming, in hysterics. She hugged the little girl, who had brown, curly hair, and told her everything would be okay. Their mother stood there in shock, paralyzed. McGuire snapped her fingers in front of the mother's face and urged her to move. Eventually she did. McGuire ran with them for about a block, but eventually they became separated.

She started to feel more comfortable the farther away she got from the finish line. Tracy was relieved that she did not hear any further explosions, but where was her husband? Seated in the grandstand, he would have been as close to the first explosion as she was. She borrowed a cell phone from a stranger. Chris answered her call. Tracy experienced a sudden feeling of relief.

So did he. "Where are you?" he asked.

"I'm two blocks away."

Chris said that he was still at the finish line. "It's nasty," he said.

Tracy would learn later that Chris had fielded her call standing in the middle of Boylston Street, looking for her, watching police shove barricades aside to get at victims, watching medical personnel carrying those same bleeding victims past him in stretchers, on wheelchairs, wondering where his wife had disappeared to after the two explosions. *Was she safe?* She was, and they agreed to meet at their hotel, the Marriott Copley. Within a few minutes they were reunited.

As close as she had come to the finish line, within the last hundred meters, Tracy McGuire is not listed as one of the finishers of the 117th running of the Boston Athletic Association Marathon. She would not be alone.

———————

Vivian Adkins, 43, an attorney from Potomac, Maryland, had run the early miles with an Internet friend, Michele Keane, who had grown up in the Boston area. Adkins enjoyed the running account Keane offered of sights passed: "Michele had been injured, I was undertrained," says Adkins, "so we both plodded along together, not caring about our finishing times." But when Keane stopped in Natick to chat with her mother, Adkins pushed ahead. Approaching the finish line, Adkins was just ahead of Tracy McGuire, although the two did not know each other.

The first bomb went off behind Adkins, who would recall: "My initial reaction was that it sounded like the howitzer they fire at the start of the Marine Corps Marathon. I next thought, why would they do that? Some overzealous celebratory stunt?" Then she saw the smoke and two yellow balloons floating skyward. It suddenly dawned on Adkins that this was not a stunt.

She ran to the right barricade near the grandstands and crouched down on the ground, rolling into a fetal position, hands over her head. Her ears were ringing. Adkins heard a second explosion. A nearby photographer frantically began to pack his gear, preparing to flee. "I knew then I was in the midst of something really bad."

Adkins got up and ran toward the finish line, aware that she could get hit any moment. She crossed the line, her chip-adjusted time recorded as 4:09:39. Walking through the finish chute, she began crying, realizing how close she had come to death. Two medical workers ran past Adkins toward the Medical Tent with a stretcher, the woman on it bleeding profusely. "I saw a trail of blood just spraying from her lower body."

The image that would remain in Vivian Adkins mind, however, was that of the two yellow balloons wafting slowly to the sky, caught in a cloud of smoke. She found this to be "haunting," because balloons were a symbol of celebration and joy. In this case, the balloons probably had been released by someone grievously injured, "the innocence of all of us going up in smoke."

Ever since their parting in Natick, Michele Keane had been trailing Vivian Adkins closely without realizing it. Keane was less than a quarter-mile behind when the first bomb went off. "I stopped, hesitated, then took another step before the second bomb detonated. People were running at me and shouting to stop, stop, stop!"

Keane moved off the course to the sidewalk near the underground garage of the Mandarin Oriental Hotel. Later reports of a bomb at that hotel would prove false. Borrowing a phone from a spectator, she called her mother and texted her daughter still at Mile 25 to assure them she was okay. Keane would confess later that, being an engineer, she reacts very rationally to tragedy. Handing the phone back to the spectator, she saw a young runner bawling uncontrollably. "She was distraught, because she had no way to get to her sister, or call her." Keane had relatives who lived only two blocks away. She invited the woman to accompany her there.

Walking to her relatives, she realized that if she had not stopped a mile earlier to hug her daughter, she might have been right in the path of the explosion, right where McGuire and Adkins had been. A lot of runners that day would reflect on "might-have-been" moments.

Looking for a second Starbucks where she could charge her dying cell phone, Sarah Mutter had walked past the site of the first explosion only minutes before and was a block away when the horror began. "My body shook. I turned and looked back and saw a huge cloud of smoke. Everyone around me had the same confused look. People were running toward us, crying, hugging each other, hysterical, tears streaming down their faces. I looked at my phone: *Dead!* Then another explosion."

Mutter reached the second Starbucks, found a wall plug and waited 10 minutes for it to charge. She ordered some tea, drank it, then realized that the Starbucks manager had begun to lock the door in response to a police order to keep everyone off the streets and away from harm. Not wanting to get stuck in Starbucks, she dodged around the manager and onto the street, wandering aimlessly toward Commonwealth Avenue.

"Do you need help?" a man asked her.

"Yes," said Mutter cautiously.

"I live across the street. Come inside. We can get you some water, food, anything you need."

Many Bostonians, who lived close to the carnage, had begun to make similar offers to dazed and wandering runners. Mutter found herself in an apartment with more than 40 other runners, strangers in a strange land, watching the news on TV, crying. "Within minutes, I had a cookie in one hand, water in another."

"Are you alone?" asked a woman.

"Yes. Kind of. I can't find my friend."

"Let me," said the woman. She borrowed Mutter's phone and soon had the friend on the line. Mutter and the friend agreed to meet at the Common, near where she had boarded the bus to Hopkinton in what seemed like an eternity ago.

Mutter thanked the owners of the apartment for their hospitality. "I walked back into the chaos. A policeman directed me toward a bus that would take me to the Common."

After collecting her bag at the Common, her phone rang. It was her father calling. A quick exchange of greetings, and her father paused: "Sarah, I didn't want to tell you before your race, but your grandmother has been very sick. She died last night."

After hanging up, Mutter dropped her bag and started crying. A woman, another stranger, saw her and gave her a hug. Sarah Mutter would remember: "She didn't know why I was crying. She didn't care. I thanked her, and she walked away."

Some of the runners approaching the line at the time of the first explosion would continue and cross that line. That included a runner wearing a bright orange shirt. His name later would be revealed as Bill Iffrig, 78, from Lake Stevens, Washington. When the bomb detonated, Iffrig went down as though struck by shrapnel. But it was the blast that knocked him off balance, causing Iffrig to trip. One of the photos that became almost a poster image for the day's events shows Iffrig on the ground, three policemen with guns drawn above him, seemingly not knowing which way to turn to confront the perpetrators. But Iffrig was more stunned than hurt. As the video clip of the chaos showed, he quickly got up and ran across the line. Having started in Wave 2, he would be given an adjusted time of 4:03:47, good enough for fourth in his age-division. Later, Iffrig was interviewed on TV looking only mildly shaken.

Also crossing the line about the same time as Iffrig was a woman, dodging around other runners. As she did so, she punched her watch to record her finishing time.

Among those closest to the blast was Dave Fortier, 48, a business owner from Newburyport, Massachusetts. In an interview with Jon Wolper of the *Valley News* in West Lebanon, New Hampshire. Fortier said that for 26.19 miles he had a fantastic time. "I saw the finish line," he told Wolper. "I thought, 'I'm going to make this thing.' "

Then came the explosion.

"The impact of the first blast forced Fortier sideways, just yards from the finish line," wrote Wolper. "Debris tore through his shoe and hit his foot. He spun around to see what had happened and cupped his left ear with his hand." All sounds afterward would be muffled. The second blast, seconds later, would sound distant. Many others close to the explosions, even if not struck by shrapnel, would suffer significant ear damage.

Fortier stumbled ahead and crossed the finish line directed by a security guard, his time recorded as 4:05:34. "I don't even remember crossing the line," he later would say. "I was too concerned looking backward down the street to where my wife and kids were located." His foot bleeding from the shrapnel, Fortier was among the first treated in the Medical Tent. He received several stitches, then vacated the tent for others more seriously injured.

Peter Sagal had guided blind runner William Greer across the line moments before. "I told him he could stop running," wrote Sagal, but Greer already had figured that out. Greer bent briefly, hands on knees, to catch his breath. Sagal put his arm around Greer's shoulder to escort him through the finishing chute. The sound of an explosion startled them.

"What the hell was that?" said someone.

Neither Sagal nor Greer could figure it out. "I had just finished my 10th marathon, my 3rd Boston," says Sagal, "and I never had heard anything like that. Never. Cowbells. Music. Cries of pain, sure. But never that."

"Keep moving please," officials shouted through megaphones, still uncertain themselves what was happening.

Mary Gorski also was in the finishing area. Her adjusted finishing time was 3:56:31. Though feeling "a little beat up," she surprised herself by being able to maintain a steady pace in the last few miles, even summoning a bit of a sprint after turning onto Boylston Street.

Gorski would write: "And there was the first blast, just behind me. Just where I would have been had I not kept up the pace."

She turned and saw smoke billowing into the air. "We thought the worst while quickly trying to think of plausible explanations: Maybe a generator blew? A gas leak? It couldn't have been a bomb. We're overreacting. It just couldn't have been a bomb."

Runners who had progressed as far as the baggage pickup area began to scramble in their bags for cell phones.

Sirens began to sound.

Kristin Stevens, 44, a dermatologist from Portland, Oregon, had qualified for Boston with a time of 3:34:09, then three weeks out became injured with plantar fasciitis, "no doubt due to over-training," she would confess. Stevens almost canceled her trip, then decided to run Boston 2013 anyway, wisely using the race as a reconnaissance mission for 2014 when (she promised herself), she would train more intelligently. Starting in Wave 2, she finished the marathon in a chip-adjusted 4:20:09. Stevens was reasonably happy. Crowd support had carried her through the most painful miles. Mission accomplished. Then:

"I was just reaching for my Mylar wrap a half block away when the first bomb detonated. I felt the explosion in my chest and smelled the smoke, but finish line banners blocked my view. Even after the second explosion, I had no idea what was happening, then runners who had finished behind me came running past, shouting, 'Run! Run!' The scene was surreal." The next several hours for Stevens, and so many others, would become, "a cold and lonely blur."

Jill Kratzer had finished in 3:41:23, well before the first explosion. She was in a changing tent with several other women. "Everyone paused for a second, then resumed dressing. It wasn't until I came outside that I realized something was wrong."

Jeanie Kayser-Jones, a professor of nursing at the University of California, San Francisco, had run Boston once before in the 1970s, but was in town mainly to support friends. She had positioned herself on the sidelines on the left side of the street, several hundred yards up from the finish line, waiting for her husband to finish. His name was Theo Jones, a retired chemistry professor from the University of San Francisco. He had hoped to break four hours, but with the clock ticking toward 4:10, it appeared that he was having an off day. Kayser-Jones walked down Boylston toward the finish line, but the crowds were too thick for her to get close. She stopped and waited, stepping up on the bottom rung of one of the barricades. She hoped to get a photo of Theo when he finished. Then the bombs went off.

"We were horrified," Kayser-Jones would explain in an email to a friend. "I began to cry and a man next to me grabbed my hand. He was waiting for his son and said he had three grandchildren in the crowd. We could smell the gunpowder."

Heather Lee-Callaghan had finished earlier. Her foot bloody, she limped through the area where she had been handed a Mylar blanket and walked over to one of the barricades to lean against it. It was not merely the pain, she was exhausted—mentally as much as physically. She began to cry. A medical volunteer approached her.

"Are you okay?" she asked.

"No," Lee-Callaghan said and pointed at her blood-stained shoe.

The volunteer signaled for a wheelchair. Lee-Callaghan lowered herself down into it to be rolled into the Medical Tent. "Every bump we hit felt like an earthquake. Every muscle in my body hurt. She lay down on one of the cots and one of the medical aides propped a foam roller under her leg and began to remove her shoe.

"If my toenail is hanging off, I don't want to see it," Lee-Callaghan instructed the aide, covering her eyes with one hand. She feared that if she saw the sight of her own blood, she might faint. The aide told her she would not lose a toenail. The blood was from blisters.

She was cold. She was shivering. Even the extra blanket they gave her did not help. "After about 20 minutes, they released me with my papers, and let me keep my disgustingly bloody sock. They suggested I throw it out, but I wanted to take a picture of it for my blog." She thanked everybody for their help, and exited the tent, planning to look for her friends at the Family Meeting Area—and, "it happened"—a tremendous boom that Lee-Callaghan felt as much as heard. She thought: *Did I just hear that?* She turned around in disbelief staring at where smoke began to billow above the finish line. Then another boom, this one more crackly and terrifying. "Smoke was towering in the air like a spreading disease of fear only a few hundred meters away. I knew in my gut that this was not going to be good."

Suddenly a lost toenail would not quite seem so awful.

Lee-Callaghan and John Munro probably were in the Medical Tent at the same time, although they did not know each other. Munro had run 3:30:22, subpar for him. Worse, he was nauseous, having thrown up on the course, dehydration complicating his condition. While waiting to collect his clothing bag, his head began to spin. "I could feel the world closing in, my field of vision narrowing, like someone pulling a curtain."

Munro knew the feeling. One time at the Rome Marathon, he had passed out to awaken in the Medical Tent. He decided to skip the passing-out part of that experience and head to the Medical Tent while he could still get there on his own. He grabbed the first volunteer, explained how he felt, and "the system took over."

A wheelchair suddenly appeared out of nowhere. Munro slumped into the chair, somewhat embarrassed at being pushed past other finishers, not realizing that since all of them were at various levels of collapse and exhaustion, they couldn't care less who was being wheeled past them. Munro would describe his medical experience:

"Upon arriving at the tent, the bar code on my bib number was scanned, providing the medics with details on who I was. I was led to one of 40 or so cots laid out in rows on either side of the tent. There was a doctor assigned to each group of a half dozen beds. The doctor took my blood pressure and stuck a thermometer into my ear to check my temperature."

As a veteran of 25 marathons, Munro had suffered most postrace problems and suggested that he was a victim of postexercise hypotension. "The doctor agreed with my self-diagnosis. My problem could be easily cured by elevating my feet, keeping me warm, and waiting until my blood pressure returned to normal." They wrapped him in blankets to combat his shivering.

Munro joked with the doctor: "Make sure to note that I was coherent."

"Don't worry," she said. "That was the first thing I wrote down."

"Thank you." Munro would note that despite there being a number of runners being administered to with IV drips, the atmosphere in the tent was "busy but good-humored," punctuated occasionally by screams of runners suffering from muscle cramps. Since it was a relatively cool day, unlike the previous year with temperatures peaking in the high 80s, it looked like the Medical Tent volunteers would have an easy day.

"Did you want to contact anyone?" asked the doctor.

Munro said he would wait, because if he told his wife, Helen, he was in the Medical Tent "again," he would be in big trouble. Eventually, he texted her of his whereabouts, and they agreed where to meet.

"In hindsight, this would be a stroke of luck," Munro would recall. "She had spent most of the day standing cheering and waving a Scottish flag near where the second bomb would explode."

John Munro lingered in the tent, sipping water, in no hurry to join the scramble outside, aware that it would take Helen time to pick her way through the crowd to their agreed meeting point. And then it happened!

"Two loud bangs," Munro would remember. "No echo or reverberation. *Bang!* Silence. *Bang!* In the windowless environment of the big white tent, there was no idea initially of what happened. Word finally filtered through of an explosion, and even then the initial assumption was of an accident.

"Then came the call to free up the beds!"

Kate Johnson had a good race, finishing in 3:39:03, a time fast enough to qualify her for next year, if she chose to run Boston again. "It was the hardest race I have run, and by far the most exciting. Only about 30 percent requalify at Boston, and I had done it!"

This was Johnson's first large marathon, so she had no idea what to expect. "There was a lot of stop-and-go to get water, snacks, a blanket, and, of course, our medals. Then we had to walk even farther to get to the school bus and reclaim our gear. I was cold and tired and ready to collapse, but still had three more blocks to walk to the Family Meeting Area."

It was then that the first bomb went off. "I didn't know what it was. Neither did anyone else. No one reacted. We just kept walking."

After finishing in 3:53:08, Terry Carella, 53, director of communications for the Cooley Law School in Lansing, Michigan, had almost reached the bag retrieval area, when she realized that somehow she missed collecting her finisher's medal. She turned and began to move her way back against the stream of finished runners. "When I finally reached the medal table, about a block away from the finish, I heard an explosion, looked up, and saw billowing smoke everywhere."

Carella looked at the woman next to her and said, "That's not good." Immediately, she heard the second explosion.

Diane DiStefano finished in 3:32:20, but then had difficulty finding her family. Everybody else seemed to be using their cell phones, but her calls would not go through. She finally reached her family and learned they were stuck on The T because of heavy marathon traffic. She suggested they get off at the Arlington Street station, and she would meet them there. After connecting, they decided to get back onto The T and travel several stations farther to where they had parked their car.

Abruptly, a transit worker informed them that there had been an emergency, and everyone needed to evacuate the station. DiStefano, still hobbling from the marathon, did not think much about what that emergency might be: "We followed hundreds of people up the stairs to the street. As we surfaced, it was immediately apparent that something had gone horribly wrong!

"Throngs of people were running in all directions. The look in their eyes was one I will never forget: a mixture of disbelief, terror, and shock. Helicopters were flying overhead, and numerous police vehicles went streaming by, lights flashing, sirens going."

DiStefano stopped a man wearing a finisher's medal. "What happened?" she asked.

The man had a blank stare. His lips were quivering. "There were explosions at the finish line. There is blood everywhere."

"Were any lives lost?"

"People must have died."

The man started to cry, then said he had to find his family. DiStefano apologized for taking his time, then turned to try to explain the tragedy to her family, still not sure what had happened.

While crossing the finish line, George Karaganis had automatically tapped his watch to record his time without looking to see what that time might have been. "I felt too sick to worry about time," he says. While he was accepting water from a volunteer, his cell phone rang. It was his sister Panagiota calling him from Athens. She had been tracking him online and informed him that his time was 4:00:46.

Karaganis thought it funny that he should receive news of his finishing time from someone halfway around the world. He shouted: "*Yes!*"

He heard the first blast and laughed again, his reaction as he turned around being that it was silly and odd for people to waste their time shooting off fireworks to celebrate four-hour marathoners. "Seeing the cloud of smoke wiped the smile from my face."

After checking her watch to see she had run 4:05:47, Pam Tymchak, 51, a stay-at-home mom from East Amherst, New York, began the typical marathoner's postfinishing routine of accepting handouts from volunteers. She recalls: "The runners all were congratulating each other for finishing when the first bomb went off. *What was that?* We saw the smoke, but could not really understand what we were seeing. Then we heard the second explosion."

Someone shouted, "Get the hell out of here!" Tymchak was not certain whether it was another runner, a volunteer, or one of the police who were running past them heading to the finish line. Some of the policemen, photos later would show, had guns drawn.

Regardless of the seriousness of the situation, none of the just-finished runners reacted. Maybe they were too tired. Tymchak says: "We began to walk quickly up Boylston to the buses to collect our bags. We were all relatively calm as we waited by the buses for our phones and belongings."

"Maybe a transformer blew," suggested one runner.

Tymchak thought: *Let's go with that.*

It was only after she retrieved her cell phone and saw the urgent texts from friends and family did Pam Tymchak begin to realize what she had witnessed. She tried to return calls, but could not get through. Early reports suggested that maybe the police had ordered telephone service cut to prevent terrorists from detonating more bombs electronically, but, in fact, the system was being overwhelmed by everyone using their cell phones.

For Kara Thelen, running the race had been a triumph: "I felt that rush of euphoria that every Boston Marathon finisher feels." She had finished in 3:44:03, a minute faster than the BQ she would need if she wanted to run Boston the following year. She followed the crowd of runners collecting food and medals, stopping briefly to check on a friend, who had felt faint, being wheeled into the Medical Tent. She met two other friends and walked with them to the buses.

"Suddenly, I heard a loud boom, looked back down the street, and saw brown smoke billowing from the sidewalk. At first, I thought the bleachers near the finish line had collapsed, but then I heard another boom and saw the smoke." Thelen and her two friends grabbed each other.

"Oh my God. There were people there," she said in horror.

Rich Benyo, editor of *Marathon & Beyond*, was waiting with his brother Drew near the baggage collection area for his wife, Rhonda, to finish. Benyo had been tracking her as she passed over the timing mats. Noting that she had passed 40-K just over four hours, Benyo estimated that she soon should finish, inevitably to appear among the masses of finished marathoners wrapped in Mylar blankets moving from medals to fluids to food to bags.

"Then it happened," as Benyo would report in the column he wrote in the July/August 2013 issue of his own publication.

Benyo realized almost immediately that the sound he heard was a bomb.

"The stream of silver-covered spent marathoners continued to move past us," he wrote. "Only a few seemed to have heard the explosion; only a few turned their heads to see what was going on back at the finish line. A few seconds later, there was a second explosion." He saw smoke rising blocks away, presumably from the area in front of the finish line.

Benyo described a nearby police car, its rooftop red lights beginning to spin. But few of the finished marathoners reacted. "Marathoners continued to move past us, some limping, most exhausted, all wrapped in silver, the occasional one stopping to look back at the now dispersing twin clouds of smoke."

One of the marathoners asked, "What's going on?"

"Bombs," said Benyo.

The marathoner shook his head as though he did not believe it and moved on. Benyo soon would learn that his wife was among the almost-finished runners stopped by police before they could enter Boylston Street. Eventually they reunited.

Karla Reppert, 38, a registered nurse from Reading, Pennsylvania, finished in 3:37:58 and had reached the buses where runners were picking up their bags when she heard the first explosion. Reppert wondered: *What was that: A cannon?* Almost immediately, she began receiving calls and text messages from friends and family checking on her safety. Puzzled, she googled: "explosion at marathon." The news already was going out to the world.

The Internet: That is how I first learned about the bombs at Boylston. Still working at home, I decided to go online to see who had won the Boston Marathon. As usual, Africans dominated the front of the field. Lelisa Desisa of Ethiopia had won in 2:10:22. Micah Kogo of Kenya and Gebregsiabher Gebremariam of Ethiopia trailed a few seconds behind. First American in fourth was Jason Hartmann of Boulder, Colorado, in 2:12:12. Among the women, Rita Jeptoo of Kenya won in 2:26:25, a half minute ahead of

Meseret Hailu of Ethiopia and Sharon Cherop. Shalane Flanagan was the first American in 2:27:08; her teammate Kara Goucher, two places behind in 2:28:11.

But which-fast-runner-won-Boston would not be the lead story in newspapers the next day. A pop-up box revealed the news that would make the 2013 Boston Marathon more than a mere sporting event.

I quickly posted what little information I had to Facebook. Then I clicked on the name of a Facebook friend "Kate Leahy." Kate was the youngest of four daughters of good friends of ours originally from Long Beach, Indiana, now living in Fort Lauderdale, Florida. I had coached Kate's two oldest sisters, Megan and Erin, in cross-country. My wife, Rose, had taught Moira, the third Leahy, in grade school. Kate was number four, the baby of the family, and I knew from Facebook postings that she and her boyfriend, David Bryant, were at Boston.

Her Facebook page appeared on my computer screen almost instantly. I breathed a sigh of relief. Kate already had posted five succinct words:

"David and I are okay!"

Some days later, I went searching for her time. Kate Leahy, 29, an engineer from Kansas City, had run 3:28:13. She and David had been walking between the Family Meeting Area and the Westin Hotel, when they heard the explosions. Still cheerful from their runs, they failed to react.

"Is that thunder?" wondered Kate.

"Can't be," said David. "It's too nice out."

Only while checking into CNN several minutes later, did they learn what happened.

My experience was typical of many runners in America. Ours is a tight community. We see each other at 5-K races. We belong to running clubs and training groups. We brush shoulders in running stores. We display copies of *Runner's World* proudly on our coffee tables. We have among our midst those superhuman individuals, the sub-elites, good enough to have qualified for and run Boston. We recognize them because they wear the gear: the T-shirts, the jackets, emblazoned with the B.A.A.'s unicorn logo. Almost all of us knew somebody who was running the 2013 Boston Marathon, or who might have been running the 2013 Boston Marathon, or had a friend who knew somebody who was running the 2013 Boston Marathon. And we worried about them, unnecessarily so, as it turned out, because the carnage was among those outside the barricades on Boylston Street: the spectators, those who cheered us, those who supported us, those who loved us, our friends and family, but also strangers who happened to show up on Boylston Street on Patriots' Day for no particular reason other than to offer someone they did not know an encouraging cheer. Several days after the bombings, I posted a short comment on Facebook saying as much. Within 24 hours, it received 120,000 views from runners who agreed with me.

Elizabeth Bunce was about to hang a medal over the head of a just-finished marathoner when she heard the explosions and saw, far in the distance, the smoke rising above Boylston Street. The medal-hanger working with Bunce, Barbie Latti, recognized immediately what had happened. "We need to get out of here," said Latti.

Bunce started to leave, then looked back and saw others on their team putting medals back in boxes, clearing the tables of boxes and moving the tables away from the center of the street to provide easier access for ambulances and squad cars. She went back to help, knowing there would be no more hugs or pecks-on-the-cheek for finishers that day.

Sandy Avila sat in the grandstands waiting for her husband, Alexis, a charity runner for Massachusetts Mentoring. "A perfect day," Avila recalled. She also was in what she described as the perfect position for taking a photo of Alexis finishing with the time clock above his head. Using her iPhone to check her husband's splits, she discovered that he had just passed 25 miles, thus should finish in the next 10 minutes.

The first bomb exploded across the street from her.

"We all were jolted, but none of us realized that the explosion was, in fact, a bomb," Sandy Avila would recall. Like many that day, the grandstand spectators were in denial—at least for a short time. "We were frightened, but thought maybe a manhole cover blew, or it was from an electrical circuit, or that some inebriated college kids were doing something stupid to disrupt the day." Then there was another explosion.

"The feeling of absolute panic set in as soon as the second bomb went off. I remember the unimaginable sound and how it shook me to the core, the overwhelming fear of not knowing if a third bomb would be aimed at those of us in the bleachers, the horror of wondering if my husband was hurt, or if he even would see me alive again.

"Everyone started screaming and running for the stairs to exit the grandstands, pushing one another out of the way. It was like a stampede. I yelled for people to calm down, so no one would get trampled to death. People were screaming and crying. Little children were paralyzed in fear. It was a nightmare. I started shaking, and that did not stop until the next day, literally.

"Once I got to the street level, I started running toward the Public Library, not knowing what else to do. I have never been so paralyzed with fear in my life, thinking that more bombs were about to explode. I froze for a moment, until a police officer screamed at me to run as fast as I could. I ran toward the Westin only to be yelled at by another officer, who told me not to keep going. I stopped in front of the Back Bay T station and tried to reach my husband by phone, only to go straight to voice mail, so I texted him. I called my sister and somehow got through to her within minutes of the explosions. Somehow, despite our phones not working any longer for calls, the text messages to each other went through. About a half hour later, my phone rang. It was Alexis, using a stranger's phone to say he was okay.

"It was a nightmare come true for all of us, but compared to those in the way of the bombs, we were the lucky ones."

After finishing, Shalane Flanagan, like most of the fast-finishing elite runners, had been steered away from the volunteers' area and escorted into the Boston Public Library. Shalane was not happy, having hoped for better than fourth. Equally bad, her time was slow, it having been a tactical race: the fast women eyeing each other rather than their watches. Then she had to endure an awkward press conference and drug testing that seemed to last forever, as is usually the case after marathons with runners dehydrated and unable to easily produce a urine specimen. Finally, success! Flanagan went to the cafeteria where all the other invited athletes were eating.

"I had just sat down to eat when I heard the first bomb go off," she later told *Runner's World*. "We all looked around. We looked out the window, but could not see anything. We were across from the finish line, but couldn't see any smoke. My husband said someone had received a text. It was a bombing. I'm not sure how many people believed him. We still thought it might have been a scaffold falling, or somebody dropping something out of a truck. Finally, someone from Hancock arrived and said we all had to move—and the person was clearly upset."

That's when Flanagan finally began to realize: Oh geez. *Something really bad did occur.*

That message finally had begun to penetrate all those near the finish line of the Boston Marathon. The echoes of both explosions had died. The smoke had blown away with the wind. The two yellow balloons long had floated away into the air. Two brothers with packs no longer on their backs had retreated to where they lived in Cambridge, a town across the Charles River. Those who had been part of the horror were still processing what had happened.

Holly Rodriguez, 36, a teacher from Portland, Oregon, shared her memories: "As I made my way back to the hotel, there was a continuous flood of sirens echoing throughout the city. Even unmarked police cars were screaming through the streets with lights flashing in their back windows. There were helicopters flying overhead and a security presence like never before."

Peter Sagal would write: "As I left Copley Square, I came across an amazing and terrifying sight. Beyond the barriers the police set up, keeping everyone away from the finish line area, I saw ambulances. Dozens of them, maybe a hundred, lined up, lights on, engines running, ready to go. It was the same terror you might feel seeing an invading army ready to launch, except instead of promising horror to come, it demonstrated that the horror already had happened."

It would take time for Kara Thelen to process what she had experienced at the 117th running of the Boston Athletic Association Marathon. Several days after arriving home, she joined so many other Boston bloggers:

"As I walked around in a daze later that evening, the events of the day played like a movie in my head. The glorious weather, the thrill of the race, the effusive spectators, the sweet finish, the explosions, the smoke, the silence, the sirens, my racing heart, my husband's familiar voice on my cell phone, the simple kindnesses offered by so many people in the aftermath.

"With a heavy heart, I realized that I'll never run Boston on a normal day again. None of us will."

14

DIASPORA

IT HAD BEEN A GALA WEEKEND FOR AMBY BURFOOT, beginning Saturday morning. Recently retired as editor for *Runner's World*, Burfoot was feted along with several other past winners of the Boston Marathon at a "Champions' Breakfast" in the Oval Room of the Copley Plaza, sponsored by the Boston Athletic Association. It was the 45th anniversary of Burfoot's 1968 victory. Among others so honored at the breakfast were Greg Meyer and Joan (Benoit) Samuelson, winners in 1983, it being their 30th anniversary. Meyer was the last American male to have won Boston.

At the Expo on Saturday and Sunday, Burfoot appeared on a panel with other members of the *Runner's World* staff on the topic: "How to Run Your Best Boston." It was a topic Burfoot had addressed at many marathon appearances. "Start slowly," he informed the crowd. "Save your strength for the uphills and downhills." Burfoot could not help thinking: *Advice easy to give, not always easy to follow.*

He and his wife, Cristina, also attended parties at the Cheers Bar, the Copley Plaza, and a restaurant named Lucca Back Bay. The couple was at the marathon in spirit, but they also were looking forward to a move later in the summer from their longtime home in Emmaus, Pennsylvania, to a new home in Mystic, Connecticut, near where Burfoot had grown up. Mystic was where Burfoot's high school coach and 1957 Boston Marathon winner, the late John J. Kelley, had lived. Burfoot had attended Wesleyan

University with two other well-known runners: Bill Rodgers and Jeff Galloway.

Despite having one foot in Emmaus and a second foot in Mystic, Boston was like a third home for Amby Burfoot. Because of duties with *Runner's World*, he attended Boston nearly every year. The 117th running of the Boston Athletic Association Marathon, he reckoned, was probably his 75th marathon overall, his 20th Boston. Burfoot's 1968 victory was relatively slow (2:22:17) because of warm weather, but later that year he achieved a PR of 2:14:29 at the Fukuoka Marathon in Japan. That was only one second slower than the world (and American) record time Buddy Edelen had set five years earlier at the Polytechnic Marathon in Great Britain.

Fortunately there was no pressure on Burfoot to run that fast this day. "Double that time and you might get it," he laughed when asked to predict a finishing time. Modestly, he had seeded himself into Wave 3, so he could run with friends John and Megan Valentine of Burlington, Vermont. John was Burfoot's first training partner back in the mid-60s. Megan was John's daughter. Previously, the three had run Boston together in 2003 and 2008. They planned to follow a pattern of four minutes running and one walking, a run/walk concept invented by his college teammate Jeff Galloway. The marathon had gone easily for the trio, but coming into the final mile, Burfoot noticed that runners ahead of them had begun to slow—then stop. His initial reaction was that celebrating college students may have surged out into the road. "There had been plenty of them in the last six miles," he later would blog for runnersworld.com.

"But the crowd didn't disperse, and I soon realized it was all marathoners, not spectators. We thudded to a stop, the road blocked ahead, and we were completely confused."

Burfoot's first thought was (which he later hated to admit): *Who's ruining my party?*

Then his cell phone rang. It was Cristina. Trailing the runners in a van, she had received a text message from Burfoot's cousin in the finish-line stands: "There have been two explosions, and the finish line is closed. The race is over."

———————

The race is over. The party is over. As word spread among runners still out on the course, also among those who earlier had crossed the finish line, not every runner understood, or was willing to accept, those words: *Bomb the Boston Marathon? How could anybody think of doing that? What was their motive?* The nonfinishers still on the course, stretching back along Commonwealth Avenue and Beacon Street all the way into the Newton hills did not want their day to end so suddenly. Many were angry. They even felt cheated.

I spent months and years trying to qualify for this race!

I raised thousands of dollars for charity to gain entry!

I trained all winter through the worst weather!

The anger of the unfinished and unfulfilled marathoners might have seemed reasonable at the time, when they were tired, stopped only blocks away from what would have been a triumphant finish. Only later, when they learned that three innocent people (a young woman, a small boy, and a Chinese exchange student) had been killed and more than 260 injured (14 of them needing to have legs amputated) would the stopped runners—like Amby Burfoot—begin to feel guilty for their thoughts.

Their diaspora had begun. Their almost aimless wandering. From many previous visits, Burfoot was familiar with side streets near the finish line and quickly made it to his hotel, the Sheraton, reuniting with Cristina, in only 20 minutes. Others would spend hours roaming the streets of Boston like "Charlie," the subject of a decades-old hit song by the Kingston Trio about a man without the necessary fare to get off The T, "the man who never returned."

Ed Geary, 58, a mechanical designer from Clermont, Florida, was one nonfinisher who may have felt akin to Charlie. He tracked his extended journey on a Garmin Forerunner 610, starting on Commonwealth Avenue, but turning left instead of right on Hereford, right on Marlborough, right again on Berkeley, right on Stuart, left on Dartmouth, right on West Newton, then one final right-left-right to his hotel, the Colonnade.

Erica Greene was at Mile 19 on the third of the four Newton hills when she learned from a nearby couple of the bombing. The two were worried about their children at the finish line. Greene was confused at first, because they still were able to run, and the spectators kept cheering. Halfway up Heartbreak Hill near an aid station, police stopped the runners. "No one knew what was going on," says Greene. When she found out, Greene was glad she was such a slow runner.

Joe Findaro had just passed Mile 23, when he got a hint of the trouble—but it was only a hint. His son Mark, running ahead, called to say he had heard about an "incident," but did not quite know what that incident might be. It took two more miles of running before Findaro learned that explosions had halted the race. "By this time cell phone service was disrupted, but a couple of family members got through, so I could report that we were safe." He saw and heard the fire engines and ambulances, then took refuge in a hotel, where he connected with other members of the Tufts Marathon team. Findaro would talk with one woman who had lost her father in New York City on September 11, 2001. He found the connection another tragic twist for an historic day.

Anita Reibel, 62, from Aventura, Florida, had been waiting at Mile 23 with her son Matt and daughter Stephanie to cheer her older son, Jake, who was running the marathon. Her husband, Harvey, had driven the pace car behind the wheelchairs and ahead of the Grand Marshals, Roberta Gibb and Sara Mae Berman. A few minutes after Jake passed, Harvey called to inform her of the explosions. "The police began telling everybody to leave the course, fearful of more explosions," recalls Anita. "Runners continued passing by, confused why all the spectators suddenly were leaving."

Somewhere between Miles 23 and 24, Kay Lynn Shanny, 50, a stay-at-home mom from Newton, Massachusetts, encountered a woman stopped in the middle of the road shouting, "The race is over!"

Her first thought was that the woman was crazy. "Everybody kept running until past Mile 25, then we were forced to stop. It was all confusion." Shanny's cell phone was almost dead, like so many others, because she had been using it to track her run. She eventually got through to her husband, Nick, who was with one son, Liam, heading to the finish line. She met them on Commonwealth Avenue, where they were joined by a second son, Brendon, who walked over from Northeastern University. Meanwhile, a third son, Ryan, climbed in a car and headed into town, only to be blocked and rerouted by Boston Police. By the time the family finally made contact in Brookline, Kay had added another three miles to her marathon adventure.

Jen Marr, running with a high school friend, almost had reached the turn from Commonwealth Avenue onto Hereford Street, when she encountered a man with his arms raised. "Stop!" he said.

Marr removed her headphones: "What?"

"The race is over."

"I don't understand."

Then she realized there were people sitting on the pavement

crying. Other people screaming. Policemen blocked access to streets that would lead to her hotel, the W Boston. "Move! Get out! Turn back!"

Her phone erupted with text messages from friends worried about her safety. Chilled, Marr was shaking too hard to answer them. She would spend the next two hours walking four miles out of her way to reach her hotel.

"But we were okay," Marr said later. "We made it." No finisher's medal yet, but Marr and her friend had made it back to their families, and that was all that mattered.

Aubrey Blanda already had turned onto Hereford when she heard the first of the two explosions. It did not penetrate. *No worries*, she thought, assuming it was from a construction site. But when she started to turn onto Boylston, she saw the cloud of smoke at the finish. That halted her. Police were running toward Blanda, telling marathoners to turn and run in the opposite direction. "Living outside New York City as I do," Blanda would comment later, "I know that when a cop tells you to turn around and run, there is no questioning his order."

Blanda stopped her watch. It showed her running time as 4:10.

A woman near Blanda apparently had seen the explosions. "She was crunched on the ground screaming, over and over. She was hysterical, completely in shock. She didn't seem to be hurt in any way, just screaming."

Blanda began talking with a woman named Charlene. She never did learn Charlene's last name. They went into a bar. Unable to use her cell phone, Blanda borrowed the bar's land line and called her husband, Philip, who was "freaking out," because he had been tracking her online and knew that she had passed 40-K at 3:57, putting her right in the line of danger.

"Charlene and I were like drowned rats. Cold, drowned rats. We started to shake. A couple of college kids gave us their jackets and got us Cokes. They all wanted to help in some way. We were in the bar for nearly 15 minutes before we finally learned a bomb had exploded. I couldn't wrap my head around that."

Janeen Bergstrom was on Boylston Street and had almost reached the Mile 26 marker when she saw both bombs explode. She did not continue to the finish line. "The police flooded the street and told everybody to turn around and head in the other direction. Everybody later would tell me that I finished, because I was so close, but a marathon is 26.2 miles, not 25.85 miles."

Later she would reflect on the day's events: "Sixteen weeks of training. All that time. All that sacrifice. Everything you do is for that moment, the moment of stepping on the mat. And it never came. But the lack of accomplishment and the emptiness I feel is compounded by guilt." Bergstrom was angry, but also felt guilty about being angry.

She had run the marathon listening to her iPod. Just before making the turn off Hereford and onto Boylston, Bergstrom pushed the forward button, searching for a song to motivate her for the final sprint. "I was searching for the theme from *Rocky*," she would recall, "but could not find it." Instead, the song she landed on just before the bombs exploded was "Stayin' Alive."

After reuniting with her family, Diane DiStefano stopped at a hotel and asked a doorman about getting a cab. "I called a cab 30 minutes ago, and it never came," said the doorman. Her husband, Aaron, used his GPS to get directions to the parking garage at the North station where they had left their car, but it was 2.5 miles away. She decided that if she could run 26.2 miles, she could walk another 2.5.

"We set out on foot, me still in my race clothes, soaking wet with a full layer of white salt from sweat covering my face. We wandered the streets of Boston still trying to reconcile with what happened." DiStefano offered two different people $50 in cash to drive them to their car, but failed to get them to agree. "I was desperate." After two hours, they reached the car and headed to the Massachusetts Turnpike to drive home to Norwich, New York. Turning on the radio, she learned that Logan Airport had been closed. The city was being shut down. "I was never so glad to be leaving a place in my life," DiStefano would say.

Valerie Petre had finished in 3:29:23. By the time the bombs exploded, Petre was back in her room in the Sheraton. Even though her room looked down on Boylston Street, she did not realize what had happened until she turned on the television set. One look out her room window convinced her that it was worse than shown on TV:

"The streets were lined with ambulances and fire trucks. Unmarked police cars with flashing lights sped up and down the road. Sirens seemed to be constant, and after a while I didn't even hear them any more. They became just background noise. Then came the military and heavily armed police, walking with their dogs. They came out of Prudential Center, marching toward our hotel. It looked like a takeover." Petre later learned that the security forces were checking the building for additional threats.

"It was like we were not in the United States, but in a Third World country."

For five hours, Kathrine Switzer had sat on the photo bridge above the finish line serving as race commentator for WBZ-TV. After finishing her duties, Switzer went up to her room in the Copley. She would write about the events that began less than an hour after she departed the finish line for *Marathon & Beyond*: "Almost immediately, the first kaboom of a bomb went off. I thought the window of our hotel room was going to burst in. Then the second explosion. The street below, filled with the sparkle of foil blankets and clinking finishers medals, of colorful, laughing friends and relatives, turned quickly into a deserted kind of moonscape as police moved confused and distressed people out and police cars, ambulances, and then very sinister-looking black vans raced in. Everything, our hotel included, went into lockdown. In just a moment, the only sound was wailing sirens." Her husband, Roger Robinson, walked in the door. "We fell into each other's arms. We were so, so lucky. Some totally innocent people lost their arms. Their legs. Their lives."

Amy Zebala, having finished in 3:38:54, also had returned to her hotel, the Lowes Back Bay, by the time the bombs exploded. "My husband, Luke, got back to the hotel around 2:55 after hearing what he thought was a car backfiring," she recalls. They turned on the TV and learned it was more than a backfire. "Our hotel was on lockdown, so there was nowhere to go. There was no chaos inside the hotel, just an eerie calm." The Zebalas ate dinner in the hotel bar with other runners watching the news. "My heart broke for those killed and injured and even for runners, who were periodically returning from the race, still in running clothes with insulated blankets—as late as 8:00 or 9:00 p.m.

After the explosions, Jim Thelen and his wife, Kara, waited in the lobby of the Park Plaza Hotel—except it was not the hotel where they were staying! The hotel being on lockdown, they could not leave. A man from Texas loaned them a charger so they could recharge their cell phone batteries. Four women from Chicago offered them their hotel room for the night if they could not get back to theirs. Seven hours after the race, they finally were released to return to their own hotel, the Newbury Guest House. After they arrived, the hotel staff ordered complimentary glasses of wine. Jim would recall: "Maybe on a normal, postmarathon day, this would not have made sense, but nothing made sense that night." Kara later told Jim that this was exactly the right touch to allow her to begin to relax after the day's tensions.

Race director Dave McGillivray was on schedule to run his 41st consecutive Boston Marathon, having arrived at Hopkinton exactly at 2:47 p.m., approximately two minutes before the first explosion. He explained what happened to Bill Burt, a reporter for the *Eagle-Tribune* in Lawrence, Massachusetts, who wrote:

"McGillivray and his friend and driver Ron Kramer arrived at the starting point at 2:47 p.m. Normally, he wouldn't remember the exact minute he arrived, but what happened minutes later will etch the time in his mind."

McGillivray told Burt: "Ron's daughter called him and told him what happened, that there were two bombs.

"My first reaction was shock and disbelief. I remember thinking, *Is this credible? Was she sure?* But before long I knew we had to return. We jumped back in the car and two state police troopers on motorcycles gave us an escort to Boston. I think we went the 26.2 miles in about 20 minutes."

McGillivray was worried about his wife, Katie, and their two children, Elle and Luke, who were in the grandstand when the first bomb exploded about 50 yards away.

"They were right across the street from the first bomb," said McGillivray. "Katie said she thought it was a burst of some sort. Then when the second one went off, everybody knew it was something very different."

Katie eventually found someone able to give her and the children a ride back to their home in North Andover. Her husband would not get home until Tuesday evening. He remained at the B.A.A. offices with a team of workers and volunteers, all of them trying to make sense of what had happened.

"After I finally got home, I hugged my wife and children," recalled McGillivray. "The first thing Luke said to me was, 'Are you okay, Dad? Are you okay?' Then he said something to me that really struck home.

"He said, 'I don't want you to direct that race any more.' "

Dave McGillivray would return to Hopkinton on Friday, April 26, to run his personal Boston Marathon and keep his streak alive at 41. When asked whether taking nearly two weeks to start and finish the marathon allowed him to maintain his fourth-place position among Boston streakers, McGillivray responded wryly, "I guess as race director, I'm allowed to make my own rules." Asked his time, he states: "11 days, 4 hours, 30 minutes." Without intending to do so, he had set a record for world's slowest marathon.

Was it possible that enough time had passed to allow us to joke, even wryly, about the events of April 15, 2013, the darkness that captured the 117th running of the Boston Athletic Association Marathon? By the time Dave McGillivray finished his 41st Boston, the two brothers who had planted the bombs had been identified, one of them killed, one of them captured after a car chase and shoot-out and police dragnet that shut down the town of Cambridge for a day. Unfortunately, one more victim was added to the list of those killed by the bombers: an MIT security guard who was sitting in his squad car in the wrong place and at the wrong time.

That could be said of all of the victims. They were not targeted by the terrorists. They were random victims, which makes the events of April 15, 2013 all the scarier:

It could happen to any of us!

The Washington Post would contact Amby Burfoot for his thoughts on the tragedy. "This was not just an attack against the Boston Marathon," Burfoot told the *Post*. "It was an attack against the American public and our democratic use of the streets. We use our public roadways for annual parades, protest marches, presidential inaugurations and, yes, marathons. We cannot cover our eyes and ears and pretend violent acts do not threaten our great institutions."

Burfoot ended: "Our institutions did not become great by following a path of timidity and cowardice. We can only hope that the Boston Marathon, though pummeled, will rise again stronger than before."

15

LOGAN

CAREY PINKOWSKI, DIRECTOR OF THE CHICAGO MARATHON, watched the women's and men's races on TV from the media center on the ground floor of the Fairmont Copley Plaza Hotel, then went upstairs to check out of his room. Returning to the lobby carrying his bags, Pinkowski exited through the main door facing Copley Square and beyond that the area past the finish line.

"Cab, sir?" asked the doorman.

"Not yet," said Pinkowski, lingering in front of the hotel, absorbing the familiar energy in the air caused by race finishers, debating whether or not to visit the finish line one more time before heading to the airport. Although Pinkowski had orchestrated world records for Chicago, he enjoyed as much watching the four- and five-hour runners streaming across the line with joy on their faces. They were his people.

But he had been in Boston three days for meetings of the World Marathon Majors (Boston, London, Berlin, Chicago, New York, Tokyo), then after a day at home with his wife, Sue, and two children, Matthew and Sarah, he would need to board a trans-Atlantic flight to spend a half dozen more days at the London Marathon.

"I'll take the cab," Pinkowski told the doorman.

"Where are you going, sir?"

"Logan Airport."

"Logan," the doorman told the taxicab driver.

With streets devoid of traffic, Pinkowski reached Logan in almost record time. Airport corridors seemed eerily empty. "There was like one person in line at security," Pinkowski recalls. The bulk of marathoners who would head home early on Monday afternoon had not yet arrived for their flights.

His flight was not until 5:10 p.m. Pinkowski headed to the Admiral's Club and called his general manager, Mike Nishi, who was still at the Copley. The time was just before 2:50 p.m.

Nishi's first comment was, "Hey, I just heard two explosions."

"What?" said Pinkowski. "Are you sure they were explosions?"

Nishi did not know. "Talk to you later," said Nishi, hanging up.

Puzzled, Pinkowski went to the bar and stared at the bank of TV sets on the wall above the coffee bar. Nothing: Just the standard soap operas and celebrity talk and game shows and reruns of old movies that one would expect to see on a Monday afternoon. Pinkowski asked the bartender to switch channels and search for any breaking news. "Oh my God," said Pinkowski when CNN's live feed filled the screen. The world was being shown the scene that would be replayed almost to the point of nausea over the next several days and weeks: Runners streaming steadily across the line with varying degrees of pain and exaltation, the clock over the finish line clicking through the numbers from 4:09:41 to 4:09:42 to 4:09:43. Then a yellow flash and a rising cloud and a runner in an orange shirt being knocked over and a man pushing someone in a wheelchair across the line on one side and a woman on the other side clicking her watch as she crossed the line, people both running away from the site of the explosion and moving toward the same site to help those injured and dying, and finally the second explosion, the camera shifting up-course to show another cloud rising, that scene also to be shown over and over and over and over and over and over again so that anyone watching TV during the next several hours, days, and weeks would have that video image burned into their memory—forever!

Carey Pinkowski suspected that when he got to London for the meeting of the World Marathon Majors, the top item on a revised agenda would be security.

Jim and Kara Thelen rose early Tuesday morning. They had a 6:00 a.m. flight from Logan Airport that would take them to Mexico for a vacation planned months earlier. The streets were dark as the couple walked to a line of waiting taxis outside their hotel. Just as they climbed into the front taxi, the driver of another taxi back in line recognized Kara as a marathoner, her blue-and-yellow jacket being the giveaway.

He called out to her: "Thank you for coming to our city!"

Departing Boston also Tuesday morning, Daniel Rideout, 53, a social studies teacher from Salem, Oregon, arrived at the airport early. He worried that the bombings might cause increased security and resulting delays. The lines at security moved slowly, but then the lines at security always move slowly. Once cleared, Rideout had time to wander the corridors, his mind swirling with thoughts related to the 117th running of the Boston Athletic Association Marathon.

Runners usually are easy to identify at Logan. They wear brightly colored clothing purchased at the Expo. They wear medals around their necks. They walk stiffly, the hills at Boston having battered their bodies. But there is a glow of satisfaction on their faces, impossible to suppress. None this day.

Rideout, however, decided that judging from runners he observed, certain newly determined rules were being observed:

1. *There would be no limping:* "The beginning of Boston Strong."

2. *There would be no boasting or complaining:* "How fast or slow anyone ran seemed inappropriate."

3. *There would be only polite eye contact:* "I don't think we wanted to observe any more sorrow."

Holly Rodriguez would wake up Tuesday morning still dazed. She and her two roommates at the Liberty Hotel went for a walk before heading to the airport, but the streets still swarmed with police, sirens continued to sound, helicopters flew overhead. There was no normalcy, or maybe this was the new normalcy.

"I didn't realize the amount of tension that my body needed to release until I made it through the long lines of security at Logan Airport. I found my gate, sat down, and sobbed—uncontrollably." Not only tears: Shoulders shaking. Others in the terminal knew the reason for her sorrow. They left her alone. Many of them were crying, too, or making brave efforts to hold back the tears.

Rodriguez was headed home to Portland, Oregon: "The next six hours were spent in flight with airplane TVs replaying the explosions over and over. Every time I glanced over to the TV of the passenger next to me and saw the explosion, I felt like I might jump out of my skin."

Rodriguez expected to be picked up by her mother, but to her surprise her husband, Michael, had come to get her. "We just held each other and cried."

Rosie Allister was among a number of runners who ran second marathons soon after Boston. She described the scene at the London Marathon one week later: "The whole field at London wore black ribbons, and there was a moment's silence at the start. Many runners crossed their heart with one hand as they crossed the finish line in triumph."

Allister would confess running the final 800 meters crying, stopping just before the finish line to applaud those applauding her and the other finishers. "Another runner who also had run

Boston gave his London medal to a child in the crowd." Allister gave hers away, too.

After arriving home, Jessica Reed discovered she was pregnant and had been several weeks pregnant at the marathon. Boy or girl, this would be her fifth child. She and Jason, her husband, decided that they would give the child the middle name "Boston." Life thus would emerge from the 2013 Boston Marathon.

Shelby Freeman Harris, 34, a clinical psychologist from Tarrytown, New York, had turned the corner onto Boylston in time to see the first explosion ahead of her. "The ground shook," she would recall. Still not certain what happened or what to do, she and others kept running. The second bomb exploded to the left in front of her. Seemingly uninjured, Harris fled into an underground garage and eventually made contact with her husband.

It was not until two days later that Harris realized the ringing in her left ear would not stop, a condition called tinnitus. She could not sleep. The ringing reminded her of the tragedy. Eventually, she adjusted to the problem, but after two weeks decided to see an ear specialist.

"I learned I had lost a significant amount of hearing in my left ear. The specialist told me my ear hears like that of an 80-year-old. He was unsure whether or not my hearing would come back."

For several more days after the examination, Harris thought about her hearing loss, the fact that she (and probably others) could be considered the uncounted victims of the Boston Marathon bombings. Finally, she decided, "If that's the worst to happen to me after being that close to the explosion—and considering the much more serious injuries of so many others—I'll take it."

By then, the identities of the two brothers who planned the horror had been revealed. It would be years before the full story of the marathon could be told. And many of the victims faced years of rehabilitation plus scars that would remain forever.

John Munro stayed several more days in the U.S., visiting Cape Cod, finding that a walk on the beach watching the whales with his wife erased some of the bad memories. He departed for home Thursday morning, offering a passport identifying him as a Scottish citizen to one of the security officers. Munro would remember the officer as being an older man with sad eyes. The security officer recognized Munro as a marathoner because of his unicorn jacket. Despite it being late in the week, there remained many walking the terminals in jackets identifying them as having run the 2013 Boston Marathon.

"Will you come back?" wondered the officer.

"I will be back," promised Munro.

Two days later at a memorial service for the three victims killed in the bombing, President Barack Obama echoed those same words: "This time next year on the third Monday in April, the world will return to this great American city to run harder than ever and to cheer even louder for the 118th Boston Marathon."

Yes, Boston, we will be back.

THE PARTICIPANTS

THESE ARE THE RUNNERS (and a few others) who participated in the 2013 Boston Marathon, listed in the approximate order in which they appear in this book, along with home town and finishing time. For those unable to finish, the Boston Athletic Association provided "projected finishing times," based on times recorded through various checkpoints. Those times are identified as: (P). Thanks to those listed below. *4:09:43* could not have been written without the full cooperation of everyone on this list.

Neil Gottlieb, Philadelphia: 3:42:47
Heather Lee-Callaghan, Timberlea, Nova Scotia: 3:37:32
Stuart Weiner, Stoughton, Massachusetts: 4:50:33 (P)
Lisa Simons Ramone: Good luck wisher
Eric Brigham, Milton, Vermont: 3:54:19
Christy Duffner, Atlanta, Georgia: 3:08:45
Gina Bartolacci, Coraopolis, Pennsylvania: 3:15:28
Whitney B. Wickes, Aspen, Colorado: 3:16:17
Alaine Perling: Spectator
Krista L. Wohnrade, Elmhurst, Illinois: 3:51:02
Kristin Reda Stevens, Portland, Oregon: 4:20:15
Peg Largo, Dewitt, Michigan: 4:05:29
William Kenneweg, Port Townsend, Washington: 3:38:50
Dave McGillivray, North Andover, Massachusetts: 11 days, 4 hours, 30 minutes
Peter McCarthy, Boston: Volunteer
Jack Fleming, Natick, Massachusetts: Media Director
George Karaganis, Athens, Greece: 4:00:36
Aubrey Birzon Blanda, Glen Ridge, New Jersey: 4:11:02 (P)
Mary Gorski, Milwaukee, Wisconsin: 3:56:31
Erica Greene, Germantown, Maryland: 5:43:44 (P)
Jen Marr, Ridgefield, Connecticut: 4:46:37 (P)
Janeen Bergstrom, Andover, Massachusetts: 4:05:07 (P)
Sarah Mutter, Woodstown, New Jersey: 3:53:35

Chris Troyanos, Norfolk, Massachusetts: Medical Service
  Coordinator
Elizabeth Bunce, Nelson, New Hampshire: Volunteer
Barbie Latti, Hancock, New Hampshire: Volunteer
Wendy Jaehn, Chicago: 3:01:47
John Bingham, Chicago: Author
Rosie Allister, Edinburgh, Scotland: 3:34:18
Kate Johnson, Lansing, Michigan: 3:39:03
Tori Menold, Lansing, Michigan: Spectator
Amy Zebala, St. Louis, Missouri: 3:38:54
Kara Zech Thelen, Grand Rapids, Michigan: 3:44:03
John Munro, Alloa, Scotland: 3:30:32
Shalane Flanagan, Portland, Oregon: 2:27:08
David Willey, Emmaus, Pennsylvania: Editor, *Runner's World*
Joe Findaro, Vienna, Virginia: 4:47:37 (P)
Valerie Petre, Holland, Michigan: 3:29:23
Michele Collette Keane, Bay Village, Ohio: 4:07:57 (P)
Jason Hartmann, Boulder, Colorado: 2:12:12
Carissa von Koch, Portland, Oregon: 3:24:58
Fred Treseler, Chestnut Hill, Massachusetts: Coach
Nancy Clark, R.D., West Newton, Massachusetts: Nutritionist
Patti Labun, Laguna Niguel, California: 3:52:12
Steven Foster, Chicago: 3:16:04
Amanda Cronin, Norwood, Massachusetts: 4:38:17 (P)
Kathrine Switzer, New Paltz, New York: TV commentator
Tracy O'Hara McGuire, Portland, Oregon: 4:09:58 (P)
Jessica Reed, Athens, Ohio: 3:36:34
Joan Ullyot, M.D., Scottsdale, Arizona: Author
Kayla Gaulke, River Falls, Wisconsin: 3:44:04
Craig Smith, Newcastle upon Tyne, Great Britain: 3:18:05
Diane di Stefano, Norwich, New York: 3:32:30
William Greer, Austin, Texas: 4:03:54
Peter Sagal, Chicago: 4:03:56
Amanda Cancellieri, Hudson, Massachusetts: 5:09:28 (P)
Stephen Mazurkiewicz, Richland, Washington: 3:07:32
Lisa Strong, Grayslake, Illinois: 4:00:21
Vivian Lee Adkins, Potomac, Maryland: 4:09:39

Bill Iffrig, Lake Stevens, Washington: 4:03:47
Dave Fortier, Newburyport, Massachusetts: 4:05:34
Jill Kratzer, Cape Charles, Virginia: 3:41:23
Jeanie Kayser-Jones, San Francisco: Spectator
Theo Jones, San Francisco: 4:15:56 (P)
Terry Carella, Lansing, Michigan: 3:53:08
Pam Tymchak, East Amherst, New York: 4:05:57
Rich Benyo, Forestville, California: Editor, *Marathon & Beyond*
Karla Reppert, Wernersville, Pennsylvania: 3:37:58
Kathryn Leahy, Kansas City: 3:28:13
Sandy Avila, Wayland, Massachusetts: Spectator
Holly Rodriguez, Portland, Oregon: 3:48:47
Amby Burfoot, Emmaus, Pennsylvania: 4:25:13 (P)
Ed Geary, Clermont, Florida: 5:08:30 (P)
Anita Reibel, Aventura, Florida: Spectator
Kay Lynn Shanny, Newton, Massachusetts: 4:36:15 (P)
Carey Pinkowski, Elmhurst, Illinois: Race Director, Chicago
   Marathon
Mike Nishi, Chicago, Illinois: Vice President, Chicago Marathon
Daniel Rideout, Salem, Oregon: 3:27:30
Shelby Freeman Harris, Tarrytown, New York: 4:07:50 (P)

ACKNOWLEDGMENTS

IN OFFERING ACKNOWLEDGMENTS to those who made possible the writing of *4:09:43*, let me first offer my thanks to those runners (and a few nonrunners) who contributed their Boston 2013 experiences. Their names are listed in The Participants section starting on page 135. Thank you, runners, for letting me quote what you wrote and tell your stories. Thanks also for your patience as I e-mailed you seemingly endlessly asking your age, your occupation, where you lived, your finishing time, and your permission to make minor modifications in your words to make the narrative flow smoothly.

4:09:43 also could not have been written without the cooperation of the Boston Athletic Association, particularly two individuals: Jack Fleming, the B.A.A.'s media director and Dave McGillivray, the B.A.A.'s race director. My wife, Rose, and I have been close friends with Jack beginning with the lead-up to the 100th running of the Boston Marathon in 1996. During a visit to Boston in June, Jack drove me the length of the marathon course. The 26-mile 385-yard route from Hopkinton Green to Boylston Street to me is sacred ground. I know I am not alone among runners in feeling this way, which is one reason why the terrorist attack cut us so deeply. Eighteen times, I have run this course as a participant in the Boston Marathon, and probably I have viewed it on almost as many occasions as a reporter for *Runner's World*, or for other publications, but the drive helped refresh my memory and inspire my writing. It was Jack who pointed out that in the last several decades Framingham, with its growing population of Brazilian immigrants, has become like a suburb of Rio de Janeiro. We also drove through Natick, where Jack and his wife live. We passed Wellesley College, although participants in the Scream Tunnel had long departed. We climbed the Newton hills, which for some unexplainable reason always seem higher and longer when traveled by car compared to when traveled on foot. (Not everybody, I know, will agree with me on this.) We stopped in a pub at Cleveland Circle for a burger and a beer with Steve Vaitones, the marathon referee. Then on along Beacon Street and Commonwealth Avenue to Boylston Street, the finish line, where it all came crashing down on our heads.

Race director Dave McGillivray also was quick with a response when I needed a question answered, such as the time of the wave starts. I became fascinated with Dave's timeline, his minute-by-minute schedule, not carried on a clipboard but in his head. It helped in writing this book that several years earlier on a writing assignment, I had shadowed Dave on race day from Copley Square to Hopkinton and back again. It amazes me that after each year's Boston Marathon, Dave returns to Hopkinton to run the course long after the runners. This permits him to keep alive his string of 41 consecutive Boston Marathons run.

Add to Jack and Dave my other friends at the B.A.A., beginning with executive director Tom Grilk. During my lifelong love affair with the Boston Marathon, I have known many of those who have kept the B.A.A. and its iconic marathon alive, beginning with Jock Semple and Will Cloney, when the race was organized out of Jock's tiny training room in the Boston Garden, and continuing under the more professional management of Guy Morse and Tom Grilk. Thanks to them the legacy continues, the flame remains lit; we will not allow the great traditions of Boston to be destroyed by a pair of bombs. It is also a pleasure while visiting the B.A.A. offices to meet again a dear friend Gloria Ratti, custodian of all the marathon memorabilia. Thanks also to Jack Fleming's coworkers Marc Davis and T. K. Skendarian, as well as to Chris Young, who worked with me in crafting the condensation of *4:09:43* that appeared in the Racer's Results Booklet, sent to all who ran Boston 2013. I was honored to be offered that assignment.

Working closely with me in presenting publishers with the manuscript of *4:09:43* in order to bring the book to market in a timely fashion, both online and in print, was Kari Stuart of ICM Partners, an agency based in New York, Los Angeles, and London. Cristina Negrón copyedited the book, catching typos and errors and making certain my grammar didn't wander off course. Bryce Culverhouse, a runner and artist I have known since he provided T-shirt designs for races I helped organize as far back as the 1980s, provided the dynamic cover design for the original eBook edition of *4:09:43*. Keith Blomberg provided the compelling design for the print edition.

Thanks also to the staff of Human Kinetics, headquartered in Champaign, Illinois. I began writing *4:09:43* without a publisher, without a contract, and without the usual access to the marketplace that my years as a published writer have taught me is necessary if you expect your book to achieve some semblance of success. I just wanted to write the story, figuring those formalities could come later. In September, Jan Seeley, publisher of *Marathon & Beyond*, had dinner with Human Kinetics CEO Brian Holding and his wife Judy. Jan told Brian about *4:09:43*, saying it "was possibly the most important running book in the last 50 years." Soon I received a call from Jason Muzinic, Consumer Division Director at HK.

I knew the publishing house well, Human Kinetics having published many important running and fitness books, among them *The Lore of Running* by Timothy Noakes and *Nancy Clark's Sports Nutrition Guidebook*. The drive between Long Beach, Indiana, and Champaign is only about three hours, so I agreed to visit, meeting with Brian and Jason and the staff, which included Bill Johnson, Rick Hollwedel, Sue Outlaw, and Maurey Willamson. Driving home, I knew I had a publisher that I could work with in bringing *4:09:43* to market, and the contract soon followed. Others who participated in the publishing and promotion of this book were Melissa Kuhl, Liz Evans, Tara Welsch, and Julie Marx Goodreau.

4:09:43 never would have been written without the continuous support over the years of my wife, Rose, who has always stood behind me during the ups and downs of my career as a writer. It must not have been easy when a few months after our wedding, I informed my bride that I was thinking of quitting my job as a magazine editor to become a full-time freelance writer. She did not blink, and it proved a fortuitous choice for us and our children and our grandchildren. Among members of our immediate family, our son David's wife, Sharon Higdon, a voluminous reader of books, offered not merely a thumbs-up after a first reading of the manuscript, but also offered several suggestions for improvements in the text. My daughter-in-law Camille Higdon provided computer-based assistance. Our daughter Laura Higdon Sandall helped with our early marketing plans.

Thanks to all of the above, but let me thank one more time the approximately 75 individuals who offered me their stories. "The 75," as I soon began to refer to them, are the true authors of *4:09:43;* I am merely the facilitator of their tales. The list of tale tellers began with Neil Gottlieb of Philadelphia, the first individual who responded to my Sunday-afternoon posting on Facebook. Neil got the first quote, but he also gets the last quote, one with which all who ran Boston 2013 certainly must agree:

"The 117th running of the Boston Marathon will always be part of me, different from the 116th I ran, and more special than so many other races over the years. This one day shaped how I approach my training, my appreciation of the gift I have been given of strong lungs and legs, but now running with a stronger heart and for a purpose, never forgetting the day that shattered the world yet brought the running community closer together forever."

—Hal Higdon
Long Beach, Indiana

Hal Higdon first became acquainted with the Boston Marathon as a member of the U.S. Army stationed in Stuttgart, Germany, training with Dean Thackwray, who would make the American Olympic team in 1956 as a marathoner. Higdon knew then that he eventually needed to move upward in distance from his usual track events (including the 3000-meter steeplechase) to the marathon. He first ran Boston in 1959, then again in 1960, failing to finish both years. "My mistake," Higdon realized later, "was trying to win the race, not finish the race."

It took five years for Higdon to figure out the training necessary for success as an elite marathoner, becoming the first American finisher (fifth overall) in 1964. En route to that successful journey, he wrote an article for *Sports Illustrated* about Boston titled "On the Run from Dogs and People" (later a book by the same title) that contributed to the increase of entrants to that race in the 1960s and the explosion of interest in running in the 1970s that continues to this day.

Higdon also wrote a coffee table book titled *Boston: A Century of Running*, published before the 100th running of the Boston Marathon in 1996. An expanded version of one chapter in that book featuring the battle in 1982 between Alberto Salazar and Dick Beardsley titled *The Duel*, continues as a best seller among running books offered on the Internet. His most popular running book is *Marathon: The Ultimate Training Guide* with a quarter-million copies sold, now in its fourth edition.

Hal Higdon has run 111 marathons, 18 of them at Boston; however, he considers himself more than a running specialist, having spent most of his career as a full-time journalist writing about a variety of subjects from business to history to science for such publications as *Reader's Digest*, *Good Housekeeping*, *National Geographic*, and *Playboy*. Among his more than three dozen published books are two involving major crimes: *The Union vs. Dr. Mudd* (about the Lincoln assassination) and *The Crime of the Century* (about the Leopold and Loeb case, featuring attorney Clarence Darrow). Thus, *4:09:43* offers a natural progression in his long career.

Hal Higdon continues to run and bike with his wife, Rose, from their winter and summer homes in Florida and Indiana. They have three children and nine grandchildren.

THE ONE FUND

AT THE REQUEST of Massachusetts Governor Deval Patrick and Boston Mayor Thomas M. Menino, The One Fund Boston was formed to assist victims and families affected by the tragic events at the Boston Marathon on April 15, 2013, and in the days that followed. Within the first two months after the marathon, through the generosity of thousands of individuals, foundations, and corporations, One Fund Boston raised more than $60 million for the victims and the families, money that went directly to the individuals who needed it. The cause continues. Consider making a direct donation to The One Fund through its secure website:

WWW.ONEFUNDBOSTON.ORG